The
Autobiographical
Consciousness

The
Autobiographical
Consciousness

WILLIAM EARLE

CHICAGO
Quadrangle Books
1972

Library of Congress Catalog Card Number: 76-116074

International Standard Book Numbers:
Cloth 0-8129-0191-6
Paper 0-8129-6164-1

For
Asher Moore

ACKNOWLEDGMENTS

I should like to express my gratitude to the American Council of Learned Societies for the fellowship it awarded me; to the Graduate School of Northwestern University for two generous grants; and to the Carnegie Corporation for a most generous grant to work and travel in Asia.

I am also grateful for permission to reprint here, in revised form, the following essays: "The Life of the Transcendental Ego," *Review of Metaphysics,* 13, no. 1; "What Is Man," *Tri-Quarterly,* Winter 1965; "Love and Metaphysics," in *Experience, Existence, and the Good,* ed. I. C. Lieb (Carbondale: University of Southern Illinois Press, 1961); "Memory," *Review of Metaphysics,* 10, no. 1; and "Intersubjective Time," in *Process and Divinity,* ed. Reese, Freeman (La Salle, Ill.: Open Court, 1964).

I should also like to express my appreciation to Mrs. Barbara Salazar for the many improvements she effected in the manuscript.

PREFACE

This little book looks for the domain of thought where wisdom may lie. For wisdom begins with nothing more than a conviction that whatever it is, it is nothing remotely resembling a science or an assemblage of correct opinions about anything. It is not, then, knowledge, if that is what knowledge is. While wisdom is compatible with the ignorance of many things, it is not itself a species of ignorance in general; wisdom, then, is not folly. Perhaps it is that form of knowledge which it is essential to the knower to know. But what is essential and what inessential? And who is the knower?

Philosophy is the traditional name for this pursuit; and if, with the ancient Greeks, we take it to be the very goal of human life and, along with politics, the absolute justification for it, we may judge for ourselves how rarely it has been regarded in this light since their time. Perhaps we have meanwhile discovered many interesting problems and their solutions—in a word, uncovered a number of intellectual curiosities—but then it may also be that the very bottom of the ancient enterprise has dropped out.

To recover the barest sense of what traditional philosophy may have aimed at, but which has often been forgotten, requires a somewhat radical reexamination of what now passes unquestioned as knowledge itself. Such is the aim of the first chapter, "Points of View." Its aim is not to attack objective knowledge, but to make room for a form of knowledge almost wholly different in form: subjective cognitive consciousness, which could possibly qualify for that form of knowledge which might be essential to the knower.

But who or what is the knower? The second chapter endeavors to define his general form. He will properly call himself "I"; and concealed within that simplest of all terms is a profoundly dialectical situation, so that the "I" is at one and the same time the subject of its *historical life* and a *transcendental* subject and agent. And so, I was born and will die; I was never born and *in principle* cannot be extinguished. The duality, which is as old as philosophy and as problematic, is dialectical in the sense that while each term of the transcendental-existential duality has meaning in contrast to its opposite, neither has meaning in isolation. But since we now seem to take it much more for granted that we are alive than that each of us is also eternal, the second chapter searches out the absolute factor in the ego, and unravels the dialectical relations between an absolute or transcendental self and a relative or existential self. Far from being separate and exclusive, the two are but abstract facets of a unity, whose career I call the "life of the transcendental ego" (Chapter 3).

If all this seems too abstract to retain any meaning at all, a second section endeavors to excavate the dialectical interplay of the two factors from the matrix of existence. Once the self that lives understands through a conscious adoption of the fully subjective point of view that its existence, precisely as it appears, is also the chance unrolling of meanings that themselves have transcendental significance, its conscious recognition of its own paradoxical but transparent life is possible. The transcendental-existential view is inaccessible to any objective mode of thought, but it is transparent to the sufficiently reflexive ego.

The second section, then, through a variety of themes, defends by concrete illustration the argument of the first section. If indeed there is a transcendental core to existence, then there can be no "doctrine of human nature," other than that which asserts that there is none. The transcendental freedom at the core of existence, and of human existence in particular, prevents any solidification of knowledge about man, his supposed nature, the laws of his life, and so on. Any proposition propounding any such thing can only be a schematization of the past history of man, invalid for any predictions. And, lest the transcendental isolation of the absolute and free ego be taken as an existential solitude, Chapter 5 seeks to show that love, at least in one definable form, is precisely the love of two absolutes creating a mutual existential absolute. Chapter 6 carries the idea further to suggest that time itself takes its origin in a present, or now, which is but another way of indicating the essential role of intersubjectivity, the mutuality of two existing absolutes, in the constitution of historical time itself. Even the phenomenon of memory (discussed in Chapter 7), when sufficiently analyzed, discloses that the consciousness of the past is possible only to that ego we have been examining, an ego that is not a series of disjunct episodes, but one that perpetually has one foot in the past and the other in the present. What could do that but a self dialectically divided between time and the timeless?

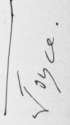

Chapters 8 and 9 consider the questions of value and morality. Here my interest is not in proposing a scheme of value or
in arguing for any specific set of values, but rather in again
pointing out that for value to be value, it must be the choice
of a transcendental-existent ego. A transcendental ego of itself
could choose nothing. A purely existent self could *affirm* nothing, but at best could desire this or that. The affirmation of
any desire is the work of the transcendental-existent ego, a
self whose existence offers existential possibilities and needs,
but whose transcendence retains its absolute freedom to affirm
or reject.

If transcendentally we retain our absolute freedom of affirmation, so that there is no transcendentally valid definition of
man or of value itself, then there can of course be no universally valid system of morality, and anything so presenting
itself is but a disguised existential choice by a man or group.
The domain of value is the domain of choice, not of logic or
knowledge; and its proper mode of discourse is not proof
or science but persuasion and example. The function of the
immorality of morality (Chapter 9) is not to demoralize but
to put morality on its own feet, so that a man can take personal responsibility for his choices, a responsibility not intelligible if he were only making intellectual errors or discovering
hitherto obscure "truths."

The two final chapters consider horror and death. The first
finds in our ambivalence toward the horrible evidence of an
ego again not wholly surrendered to existence but caught in
the irony of both loving and hating it. Death presents the final
irony: while the transcendental ego desires to live, if it does,
that very life it desires is nevertheless dialectically dedicated to
its own disappearance; who could wish it prolonged forever,
and at which particular time of life?

And after death? Has the timeless ego any possibility of

recuperating what it has all been? This chapter will have to wait.

But perhaps enough has been said to make plausible the initial contention, that by assuming, through subjective reflexivity, that vantage point which each of us occupies in any case, it might be possible for us to recover our own existences, unpredictable lives played out within transcendental horizons that enclose absolute chance, and approach that knowledge which is essential to each of us, because it makes us what we are.

CONTENTS

The
Autobiographical
Consciousness

PART I

Terms and Methods

1

Points of View

"Know Thyself"

THE QUESTION "What is philosophy?" is perhaps one of the most frequently asked in philosophy, and almost as frequently one of the most sterile. The question expresses the perpetual crisis of philosophy; and perhaps to a bystander, the spectacle of philosophers asking themselves what they are doing seems ludicrous, much as if architects were first to conduct an interminable debate on what architecture was before setting to work. And philosophers themselves weary of their perpetual self-examination and become more than a little testy about it in an age when the very ideal of philosophy seems valueless. But the fact is that everyone is increasingly becoming a bystander, even the philosophers themselves. And yet not many would wish to suppress philosophical thinking. But what is it?

Everyone knows what it is. Its definition was given by the

5

Greeks: the love of wisdom. But what is that? Socrates, we all remember, said that the only thing he knew was that he knew nothing—not a very promising beginning or ending until we also recall that the oracle said he was the "wisest man in Greece." Pigs don't know anything either, but no oracle has declared them wise. Socrates' oracle also enjoined man to "know thyself." And so philosophy as the love of wisdom is at the start involved in a paradox. Socrates, the "wisest man in Greece," said he knew nothing, nothing of what was "above the heavens or below the earth"; and yet the same oracle that urged us to know ourselves declared him to be wise. Evidently the oracle felt that wisdom did not lie in knowing about what was above the heavens or below the earth, but rather in knowing something a good deal closer to the knower: himself. Philosophy, in addition, was not said to consist of the possession of such knowledge, but rather its *love,* which to the Greeks meant not so much a distant admiration for a beautiful thing as the striving for its possession.

But all this may be of merely philological interest. It certainly appears so when we take even the most casual tour through the later history of what has been offered as "wisdom." Virtually every knowable subject has been offered up as the focus of wisdom. Wisdom has been identified with formal logic; with the study of the methods of the sciences; with the study of language; with a kind of general natural science of what is "above the heavens and below the earth"; with "value theory," the theory of knowledge; with a metaphysical analysis of those categories that everything must exemplify; and even with its own history. And while it is perfectly possible to take an interest in any of these studies, it can also be asked whether better and wiser men than ourselves have not been ignorant of the results of these studies, and whether worse men than ourselves have known them. In short, the history of philosophy presents us with the image of a restless oscillation around a concealed axis; and no matter how "interesting" such studies may be, they have no initial right whatsoever to be identified with anything that Socrates would have called philosophy. In short, they may be intellectual curiosities. Their value may be not intrinsic, but at best instrumental. They proceed out of their own concealed source, and it is to that source that their value, if any, must revert. And what could that concealed source be but ourselves, which the Delphic oracle at the beginning enjoined us to know?

Wisdom of course is a lofty thing, and "only the gods have it," as Socrates said. But knowledge looks like something a little more within our grasp, though what we then have may turn out to be something of no demonstrable value. But even on the surface of it, the opposite of wisdom is folly, whereas the opposite of knowledge is ignorance; these are not the same things. No one is content to think himself a fool, and yet everyone is perfectly content to remain ignorant of most things that are or could be known. They are unimportant, we say, and indeed they may be; but then what *is* important? Socrates declared that the only thing he was interested in was the "good." So at the beginning, philosophy was never taken to be simply knowledge, or even knowledge of very general things, but, since it was the "love of wisdom," an aspiration toward that knowledge which it was *essential* to know—and to whom could it be essential but the man aspiring toward it? And what kind of knowledge was that? "Know thyself"! But Greek oracles never gave anything but ambiguous answers, answers whose interpretation depended on the hearer and which were therefore as much questions as answers. Today we are hardly in a better position than the Greeks to interpret the oracle; we certainly have many more foolish responses to it than they did. In short, we remain today

in precisely the same position as the Greeks, stung by an
absolute commandment that directs us on pain of being foolish
to a task that is radically ambiguous. No wonder philosophy
lives in a perpetual crisis over what it is, and no wonder we
settle for something a good deal less pretentious than the
love of wisdom.

How indeed am I to know myself? Through psychoanalysis?
By asking someone else? By asking myself? If I did manage
to achieve any such knowledge, how could I confirm it? Are
there public or experimental means of achieving warrantable
assertions about myself which would constitute the desired
knowledge? What sort of thing would I know if I ever suc-
ceeded, even in part? And am I the sort of thing that *can* be
known? Is what I am looking for really knowledge at all? And
doesn't the whole project verge on the narcissistic? Why
should anyone else care? Why should I not begin and end
with trying to know others? And why indeed are those mag-
nificent things "above the heavens and below the earth," the
subjects of the natural sciences, not to be included in philosophy? Compared with them, is not the whole human scene a
rather temporary and miserable phenomenon? If the natural
sciences present us with an astounding panorama of what the
cosmos has become, that out of which we have emerged and
back into which we die, isn't the injunction to "know thyself"
an invitation to restrict our minds to the most narrow of all
possible subjects, ourselves?

This essay seeks to offer some suggestions on this general
theme. Its preoccupation will be the circumscribing of that
"knowledge which it is essential to the knower to know."
Needless to say, it does not aspire to offer that knowledge, but
only to discover its domain, to point toward that region where
essential knowledge may be found. It is, then, one more effort
to redefine philosophy, and by procedures that, no matter how

sound the argument may be, are themselves merely negative, preparatory, and, in the long run, dispensable.

The outline of the argument is simple enough, although its defense and its ramifications may have to be somewhat elaborate. If we are looking for the domain of that knowledge which is essential to the knower—a knower, moreover, who is himself *singular* and *existent,* one who was born and will die and is not "humanity" or some "community of scientists or scholars"—then (*a*) such knowing cannot be either of or through the universal. For if what I knew of myself were only those universal laws or principles I exemplified, then even if my thought were true, it would ignore my singularity by knowing of that singularity only that which was "predicable of many." "Knowing thyself" therefore must not be some form of knowing a universal "thyself" or *any conceptual cognition* at all, but rather a reflexive elucidation of the singular being that I am. Nor (*b*) can any such self-knowledge be properly characterized as objective knowledge. It cannot be objective in the sense of knowing an object, me, since any object as such is in essence precisely that which is *not-me,* the subject; to know a subject as an object is to know it as what it is not. Nor can self-knowledge be objective in the scientific sense, a knowledge that depends for its truth and validity on confirmation by other subjectivities. Whatever self-knowledge may be, it cannot be an opinion about myself that can be substantiated only by public agreement. If it were, the opinion in question might very well be confirmed by others, and thus be "true," but the truth of it would not necessarily require *my* confirmation, assent, or cooperation, and therefore could not essentially implicate my existence. What I need to know, therefore, cannot be some correct opinion about myself or some hypothesis about me with a high probability index. I, the existing singular subject, must be the subject of this cognition and at the same time must be necessarily implicated in its truth. And (*c*) while science and certain theoretical forms of philosophy look for *explanations* of phenomena, "Know thyself" does not enjoin me to find explanations of myself, if finding explanations means finding causes for myself in what lies outside myself, in what is *not* me. "Knowing" is not necessarily explanatory, but it might be regarded as elucidation: that is, raising to explicit, reflexive consciousness that which is already implicitly grasped. It might be an effort to excavate the implicit, buried sense of the existence of a singular being by that singular being—in a word, the "autobiography" of the singular being. "Know thyself" invites me to become explicit as to who I am, what it is for me to exist; what my singular existence has been, where it is now, and what lies before me. "Ontological autobiography," we shall call it, with no particular emphasis upon its "graphical" or recorded character; it is a question of a form of consciousness rather than of literature. Why the qualifier "ontological" has been added will, I hope, become clearer when we have analyzed in more detail the character of that which can have an autobiography.

Since the universal, objective, and explanatory have such deep roots in our habitual conception of knowing, as if they defined knowledge itself and not merely one of its forms, and since the singular, subjective, private, and intuitive are consequently seen as synonymous with the unknowable, trivial, fanciful, or egotistical, it may be worthwhile before we go any further to turn our attention to a systematic examination of forms of knowing. "Know thyself" is certainly a form of knowing, but a form that fits very poorly into traditional ideas of what knowing must be.

Philosophy and the Universal

For a large and continuing part of the philosophic tradition, knowledge *inherently* depends upon the universal or "concept." Aristotle defined what we call the universal as "that which is predicable of many." There need not be any existing individuals of whom it can be predicated, but it still is the sort of thing that one might predicate of a plurality of instances. When we know anything, we either know something about these universals themselves, as when we know that circularity is different from triangularity, or we know singular things *through* these abstract universals, as when we know that "this plate is circular." Let us confine our attention to the latter kind of knowledge, the knowledge of existent singulars through the universals they exemplify. The typical form of such judgment is: this (singular) is such-and-so; that is, this falls within a certain class or is subsumed under a universal that describes it, an abstract property. And if such a subsumptive judgment is the typical expression of what we know, it seems clear that knowledge as such is the subsumption of the singular under the general or universal. Only when the singular is subsumed under the universal can it be "known"; that is, it is known under whatever universal or common name subsumes it correctly. Hence, declarative propositions, in which we say what we know, are typically propositions in which the subject term, which may be a proper name, is subsumed under the predicate term, which is typically a common noun. "Fido is a dog"; he is included in the class of dogs—all those that share the common, universal characteristic that defines dogs as such. And now in this form *and this form alone* we are supposed to know Fido, the singular dog.

As a consequence, it is frequently thought that if we were to deprive ourselves of these universals or common nouns we would no longer really know anything at all, but would simply be bombarded by singularities that would be unrecognizable since they were not subsumed under universals, bare particulars without any determinate nature. In this vein falls Kant's famous dictum, "Intuitions without concepts are blind; concepts without intuitions, empty."

That nothing of the sort is true is apparent, I believe, upon the slightest reflection. If the singular that is "intuited" were itself devoid of a determinate nature—that is, if its intuition were "blind"—it would of course be impossible later to know under *which* universal or common noun to subsume it. Or, again, if knowing what a singular is means recognizing its similarities to other singulars, it is clear that knowing could never get started; for how am I to see that this looks like that if this, in its first appearance, is wholly without determination? Recognition is, of course, precisely a re-cognizing; but re-cognizing is not necessary for cognizing, and in fact obviously depends upon a primordial act of cognizing: intuition. Intuition is never blind and never needs the eyes of the concept to see.

We can, then, judge a singular to fall under a universal or to be a member of a class of similar things only if that singular is itself already determinate and seen as such. It hasn't the slightest need of either an abstract universal or a class of similar things to appear to us as what it is, a determinate singular. None of the intuitive functions of consciousness, memory, imagination, perception, and so on waits in blindness for the light of the universal; each act grasps its own determinate and singular object immediately, without having to be detoured up through abstractions, only to be redirected down eventually to its appropriate singular object. As Schopenhauer remarks, such a procedure is like never drinking water directly from the well, but drinking it only after it has passed through an interminable aqueduct.

What then is the *purpose* of these subsumptive judgments? So far, they seem to be an idle duplication of what is already present in intuition. Perhaps their most important function is communication. The universal or common noun serving as a predicate directs the attention of the hearer to what the speaker has before his mind, to its "class." If I say, "Fido is a dog," I say it to someone who does not know Fido and to whom Fido is absent, under the assumption that he has seen other dogs and therefore can understand that Fido is something like them. On the other hand, it would be absurd for me to announce that "Fido is a dog" if Fido were right there wagging his tail, nor would anyone ask. Or if someone asked me, "What is that?" it would only be because *that,* whatever it was, did *not* disclose to his perception what it was. Perhaps it is a new tool. My answer, in the form of a subsumptive judgment, would declare it to be similar to things he was presumably familiar with. Or, better, I would show him how it worked, thereby avoiding concepts altogether. To assume now that knowledge is inherently a subsumption of singular things under universals, that it is judgmental rather than intuitive, is to assume that we must constantly talk to ourselves and others and that without such speech we would remain blind or ignorant of what was before our very eyes.

The subsumptive judgment, then, has a function for communication: someone can tell me that something I do not see or am not acquainted with is like something I am acquainted with. Useful enough, but it should never be turned into a *condition* of knowledge unless knowledge is *always* to be about what we do not see and are not acquainted with directly— clearly a self-defeating ideal. *Somebody* must see things directly and in person if he is ever going to tell us, who do not see them, what they are like.

So the first prejudice to be disposed of is the assumption that the singular is indeterminate until it is qualified by abstract or universal predicates or, equivalently, that the intuitive powers of consciousness, those that direct themselves to the concrete and singular, are blind until "reason" with its concepts cooperates to tell intuition what it is intuiting. If the singular is perfectly capable of being grasped by the intuitive powers of mind without the universal, this does not mean that the singular does not *also* exemplify a universal; to be sure, it must, but this hardly implies that the singular is either unintuitable or itself indeterminate until its appropriate concept or universal is found.

Second, if knowing means knowing the singular *through* the universal—that is, the laws and principles that the singular exemplifies—it seems clear that while in this fashion we see something of the singular, we also miss something of it. Cognition through universals must inherently miss precisely that which distinguishes singulars from universals: their singularity. Now this might seem to be a trivial loss, as indeed it is for certain types of knowledge and certain uses of knowledge. A natural scientist as such could hardly care less about the singular natural thing he observes or experiments on; it is only as it represents others of its class that it is useful to him. And so when Fido has been experimented on and has yielded whatever general truth he can, he is discarded. Natural science pursues the universal and the general; it seeks laws and principles, and the singular functions for it only as the exemplification of some possible law or principle. And, having secured some general principle, science becomes practical or applied by returning to the individual, but only insofar as that singular individual conforms to or deviates from the principle. This is the sort of circuit of thought that operates in the natural sciences, and it seems appropriate for its subject matter and purposes.

But the question is immediately raised whether such a cognitive attitude is not inappropriate to other domains that do not fall within the scope of the natural sciences or their practical uses. For if the universal, in whatever form, is that which is repeatable, that which is "predicable of many" or the "one among many" sought by Plato as knowledge—that which is the abstractly intelligible and the foundation of all "necessary" truths, such as those of mathematics and logic—then it must be a remarkably inappropriate means of grasping in reality that which is unrepeatable, singular, contingent, and free; in a word, the existential domain of human life. If Tom invites Dick and Harry to a party, while it is true that each is a man, it is not to exhibit *that* universal that they are invited; Tom by himself would suffice for that purpose. Nor are they invited because they exemplify any other set of universals, no matter how closely that set may come to describing Dick and Harry. Tom invites these singularities as singularities, and therefore issues his invitation to singularities with *proper names*. It can hardly be by accident that persons in their everyday associations address each other by proper names and express themselves by "I." While it is true enough that the term "I" can be and is used by everyone, and therefore looks like another universal, it is not as a universal that it is used, but rather as a means of expressing the radical singularity of each particular person. The term acquires this function only in its actual employment or utterance, and not when abstracted from that employment, as in a dictionary. We shall return to this point later. For the moment it is enough to note that the speech *of* and *in* existence is not speech *about* it, nor is it intelligible in abstraction from its actual employment; its sense is given only in its actual usage, and in that usage it is much more a question of expression, address, persuasion—performance, in short, a form of existing action itself—than a matter of subsumptive propositions about existence which have objective validity. Nor does language in this role sink to the unintelligible and uncommunicative simply because it does not say what it has to say in the form of objective propositions about things. To speak in any fashion is to say something, and all forms of saying something are modes of elucidation, even when all those modes are not in the style of the declarative proposition *about* objects.

In its own obsession with the universal, philosophy has frequently been driven to an aspiration to know the most universal things of all: the transcendental conditions of being, knowing, or saying—conditions that are supposed to make any particular being, particular truth, or particular utterance *possible*. But even if we should grant that some such knowledge were possible, it would remain an open question whether its possession were precisely what the Greek oracle commanded, or, as Kierkegaard might have put it, whether it were not instead the opposite, a *distraction* from the concerns of a "subjective thinker," a flight to just those things it is *not* essential to know.

Plato, following this transcendental lead, praised the philosopher as the "spectator of all time and existence" and found some good-natured sympathy for Thales, who fell in a ditch while watching everlasting stars, as if the stars were nobler than Thales himself. And throughout a good part of the tradition, the philosopher was expected to be absent-minded toward others, forgetful of himself, ignorant of what every other man knew but knowledgeable about other things, those transcendental conditions of being, knowledge, or speech. If his own being, knowledge, and speech were themselves sometimes rather pitiable, he was still to be praised for the "loftiness"—that is, the universality—of his aspiration. He knew principles, but was expected to be ignorant of their "mere application." His own life and person as well as the lives and persons of those around him were matters of indifference to him; he lived in "another world," he kept his eyes on that which was universally true of all men and times and places. All that he was and all that existed about him were after all only temporary illustrations of what must be true everywhere. He never hurried, as Aristotle remarks, for what was worth hurrying toward? He was indifferent about his dress, for, as Spinoza says, why put beautiful robes over a worthless body? Why robes should be judged more beautiful than the body is left to our conjecture. In any event, the aspiration to grasp what is forever and universally true, the transcendental "grounds" for all things, emerged as one typical human project called "philosophy." It has most certainly produced minds of a very high order, but we still cannot say whether it is the same as wisdom, or whether it is not rather the opposite of wisdom.

Nietzsche: "Against the value of the forever unchanging . . . the value of the briefest, most perishable, the most seductive glints of gold on the belly of the serpent, *vita.*" [1] The "forever unchanging"—it is not said that there is no such thing; it is its *value* that Nietzsche questions. Can the unchanging "background," the transcendental conditions or the universal, be of such a sort that an "interest" can be taken in it? If the universal is what in principle is repeatable, what about that which in principle is unrepeatable—our lives as we live them and as they are for us, and not as they are in their roles of transient diagrams of timeless principles? Though philosophy has al-

---

[1] *Wille zur Macht,* #577.

ways tended to regard anyone's personal life as of "merely autobiographical significance," would it not be *radically absurd* for any existing man to look upon his own life in any such fashion? The "thinker's thought must be independent of the thinker's life" if it is to achieve universality; but is there not another form of thought that in principle is not merely *dependent* upon the thinker's singular and personal life but *identical with it,* and would this not be "autobiographical"? Needless to say, that thought could hardly be about the same subject matter as thought that can be called universal, nor could its aim be the same. It would therefore be a radical mistake to suppose that the value of ontological autobiography would be in the contribution it makes to our knowledge of something called "mankind"; that is just what it does not, cannot, and should not aspire to do. It might, however, have the value of being essential to the singular man himself; and since that is what each such thought always is anyway, the service it offers could hardly be trivial.

Philosophy and the Objective

Objective truth is another "idol of the tribe" worshiped to the extent that it seems to its lovers synonymous with truth itself. The work of Kierkegaard should have been sufficient to warn us against this delusion, but frequently his own defense of "subjective truth" and its "subjective thinker" has itself been turned into one more purportedly objectively valid "doctrine," and in that guise has been guilty of wild and uncontrollable consequences. I shall limit my own argument to suggestions that "objective thought," and with it "objective truth" and its impersonal thinker—in a word, science and its scientist—are but limited domains of the whole, and that to whatever extent philosophy aspires to the condition of science, it has abandoned its hope of being intrinsically important to the thinker.

What, then, is objective thought? Altogether, perhaps it can be described by its method and its theme: it is that mode of thinking which deals in a *publicly* verifiable way with "objects" that are independent of the thinker and his thought. "Objectivism," then, would be the general thesis that truth is to be had only through those intellectual procedures or methods that are in principle publicly or intersubjectively testable, and which deal only with that which can stand before us as some sort of "object." If not everything that exists can be brought before the mind as an "object," and if there is a mode of thought that can be true but which is not in principle intersubjectively confirmable or publicly testable, then the *general* validity of objectivism requires radical qualification.

What precisely is an "object"? In this discussion, I have something more general in mind than the usual "substance" or "thing." What I mean by the term is anything whatsoever that can *stand before* the mind as its *explicit theme.* Hence I include not only material things in the usual sense, but also their properties, their movements, their relations, their quantities, and their forces, as well as what we might call "ideal objects"—universals, abstractions, principles, or laws held either to describe events or to govern them. From this informal list, it can be seen that "objectivity" as I conceive it implies not merely a contrast to "subjectivity," but a relationship to it; to be an "object" is to be an object *for a subject;* nothing can, strictly speaking, be an object *in itself.* Objectivity places a something-or-other before some subjectivity for and to which it is objective. And yet anything that could possibly become such an object for a subject must necessarily *also* be a something in itself. Loosely, it must have some reality independent of the subject, although it is not in *that* respect that

it is an "object." Phenomenologically, the mind must consider
everything present to it "objectively" as (*a*) a reality *independent* of the subjective act considering it and (*b*) dependent
upon that act for its status of objectivity to it.[2]

Thus every properly so-called intentional act aims at or envisages some objectivity that is *other* to that very act; perception perceives the perceptible thing and not perception itself;
desire desires the thing desired and not desire itself; fear
fears the fearful and not fear itself; conceiving conceives a
conception and not conceiving itself, and so on. In this sense,
acts of consciousness aim at objectivities distinct from the acts
themselves. Mind in this respect is perpetually concerned with
or perceptive or cognitive of objectivities that it takes to be
"other," independent realities that are somewhere and somehow "out there" and which somehow constitute a presumptive
"world." And yet this very independence of or objectivity to
me, the subject, is a status conferred upon them by me and
unthinkable without some me.

These two general features defining the very essence of objectivity at the same time enable us to perceive its *essential
limits*. Objectivity cannot then be identified with being, but
represents only a circumscribed domain within it. Correlatively,
objective consciousness that concerns itself with such objectivities cannot be identified with consciousness itself; nor can
objective truth be identified with truth itself. With regard to
objects themselves, nothing can confront me as the theme of
my attention except as a finite, delimitable something-or-other
against a *background* of *essentially correlated* finite objects.
For any given thematization, it is the object that occupies the
foreground or which becomes "objective," while its correlated
background remains implicit, understood, presupposed, tacit.

---

[2] See my *Objectivity* (Chicago: Quadrangle Books, 1968).

As the thematization shifts, what was formerly concealed in the background may be brought forward as a new object while the first sinks back into the new background. But always each object must be a finite determinate something-or-other discriminable from other finite determinates. This situation has been widely studied by Gestalt psychology, of course, in the context of perception; but the same general situation pertains to all possible objects and their objective domains. Each intentional act aims at a finite object in a "world" that includes both that object *and others*. Hence memory recalls a past event out of the world of that past event and rejects other past events. Desire aims at some specific desired object and not at some other object that might be desired in the world of desired objects. Ideal thought conceives of an ideal object and rejects another, all in the ideal world of such ideal objects, the world of ideal possibilities whose structure includes presupposed, implied, and correlative ideal objects or "essences." And so each type of object has its essentially correlated type of world within which it has provisionally emerged as an objective theme for me by my act of directing my consciousness to it.

Perceptual objects always exist within a world of other possible perceptual objects; future objects in their own future world; ideal objects or "essences" in their own appropriate ideal world of co-implicated ideal objects. And yet the world of each type of object can never itself become an object, for each act of consciousness takes place within a horizon of consciousness, which contains the finite object to which I now attend but blocks from my view the infinity of objects that might be seen from other vantage points. Nor can the horizon itself become an object, for if I move toward it in order to look at it too, it only shifts elsewhere, accommodating its flight to my own. The world of perceptual objects, then, is not limited to the objects visible to me as I stand here, for there is nothing to prevent me from moving closer to the horizon, which then shifts to bring other objects within my view. A horizon circumscribes that portion of a world which I can apprehend from some specific "here"; it thus is always provisional and always carries the implication that there is more beyond it. The "here" is my actual finite thematized object; its horizon is the limit of visible background; its world is the infinity of all possible horizons.

At the beginning, then, two domains, necessary for the very sense of object itself, *cannot* become objective: the horizon of that object and the world within which both object and horizon have their senses. And since both horizon and world are necessary correlates of object, yet are never themselves capable of being given as objects, we have an argument for the constitutive role of the *transcendental ego* in giving meaning to its own objects. Since neither horizon nor world is in principle capable of being given as an object, the source of these "meanings" must be elsewhere than the given; and where could that be except in the transcendental ego itself, whose structure we are about to see includes precisely that infinity and absoluteness which are essential to the meanings of horizon and world? If meaning does indeed reside in the ego, "objects" as a class must necessarily imply not only meaning, but horizon and world, which are not themselves objects but meanings, with their source in the absolute ego, which interprets things as things-in-a-world. The domain of objectivity, then, is not exhaustive of either meaning or being; in this sense, objectivity itself necessarily implies that which is not objective. At this point, phenomenology rejoins Kant: if the question is asked whether the world of "objects" is independent of subjectivity, the answer is "Empirically, yes; transcendentally, no." Or: Is anything *absolutely* independent of subjectivity? "Transcendentally, yes; empirically, no." Perhaps the whole matter would become self-evident if we were to consider what would happen if the world *were* to become an object for our perception; we would then be forced to ask, "But where *is* it?" and would be forced to posit yet another world within which we had perceived the first. But there can be only one world; and that truth is self-evident, since the functional meaning of "world" is not a given datum or empirical fact to be observed or subjected to experimentation, but rather the work of ourselves, transcendental egos: a significance given by the ego to certain of its data in order to interpret them as presentations of things-in-a-world.

But even among what are frequently classified as objects, some seem to lose their "objective" character upon closer scrutiny. The most puzzling of these is the large class of *motions and actions,* what Plato called "becoming," coming into being or passing out of being, or changes of any sort. And the simple question is how anything can be an object for me unless it is already constituted; that is, finished or made up as what it is. How can what does not yet exist or what has not yet appeared to me be an object now for me? And yet this is exactly the situation that obtains with respect to any motion or action *while it is taking place.* For while the action is in progress or the moving thing is moving, it is not yet finished; neither the action nor the motion is yet constituted, but is rather in the act of being constituted. How then can any such thing become for me an "object"? Not being finished, it is not all there *to be thematized.* If I fill out my perceptions with retentions and anticipations, I can add to the changing present some determinate content; but what I add is no longer what is, but what *has been,* the finished past or a presumptive future. Action in the present is in the act of constituting itself, a constitution that will be completed only when it all is in the past.

Becoming in general then can be an object for us only on pain of losing its very quality of becoming and changing into an ideal construction of memory or anticipation. Now since *subjective* existence exists only through acts, if we were confined to an objectifying consciousness, we should be in principle incapable of being conscious of our own actual existence, let alone the actual existence of other things and persons. The truth is that the entire domain of "objectivity" represents a systematic but ideal construction of consciousness; its favorite objective terms point to ideal things constructed out of a flux that is inaccessible to it, implying a horizon of similar things in a world of objects, both horizon and world being themselves further ideal constructs.

It is not my purpose to consider this side of things further here; if even the objective world discloses upon analysis that it is not exhaustive of being, the domain of subjectivity itself offers an exception that is closer to our present interests.

For if nothing can be an "object" *for* us unless it is other *to* us, it follows that *no ego can objectively apprehend itself as itself*. To be an object is to be an objective *other* to some other; but the ego apprehends itself as the *same* as itself. Now, of course, it might be possible for a subject to apprehend something objectively which turned out to be the same as itself; but it could not apprehend it *as itself* as long as it apprehended it objectively. The objective apprehension of oneself *as though* one were another describes what *seems* to occur in cases of profound schizophrenia or alienation; but it can hardly be laid down as an *a priori* necessity for all apprehension. As Descartes made explicit, every time I reflect upon my own thinking, I am certain that I am. But this is my own thinking, and not my objective thinking about another's thinking, or some entertainment of my own thinking as though it were the thinking of someone other than myself, the one reflecting. And so indeed it is obvious that I am certain of my existence, and it is equally obvious that I could not ever be certain of myself if I were to restrict my consciousness to its objectifying forms. The slightest reflection is sufficient to show me that my own awareness of myself is immediate, that it never then appears to me as the thinking of someone else or anything that could possibly be the thinking of anyone except myself, and that while I am unaware of the origins of my thinking, I am certain that it is indeed mine. Further, my reflection itself is sufficent to convince me that the thinking or consciousness upon which I am reflecting is concurrent with my act of reflection. I know that I am conscious at the very moment I am conscious. "Reflection" sometimes has the sense of a retrospective glance over what I have just been thinking; but while this is obviously possible, reflection is hardly confined to materials furnished by memory, for the very doubtfulness of any specific memory would render my reflective certitude of my present existence impossible. And so: I am certain of my present conscious life, and this certitude is normal and indubitable. I have an immediate or intuitive reflexive grasp of my own consciousness and I grasp it *as mine*. All this would be logically impossible if we were confined to an objectifying consciousness. If then I should ever wish to "know myself," it is certain that such knowledge would not be either an objectification of myself or necessarily a memory of myself. These other modes of consciousness must all find their places and utilities; but neither is nor can be primordial.

And so it is clear that the domain of objectivity is merely one out of the whole, but even within this domain objects inherently demand to be located within their proper horizons, which are not themselves objects; and that from the domain of objectivity we must eventually exclude every form of becoming —an exclusion that would throw out life, action, and movement in the bargain—and every form of self-consciousness, since no ego can be an object for itself. The truth is that far from being equivalent to being, objectivity as a domain represents a tentative, constructed, and fairly limited area of being. In any event, it must on essential lines exclude *everything* that we are interested in here.

But "objectivity" is not merely the name of a limited domain of being; it is also a certain stance, position, or attitude of consciousness. Specifically, objectivity is that stance of consciousness in which it is intentionally turned toward what is not itself, some other that is its object. Since that other is other to my consciousness of it, it acquires an "independent reality," independent in relation to my own flux of consciousness. The paradox of these relations need not detain us long. All objects of consciousness are both logically *dependent* on consciousness, or they would have nothing to be other *to;* and yet also *independent* of consciousness, since that is what grounds their otherness. In their independence, their "empirical reality," they imply further developments in any consciousness that may wish to be conscious of them. Thus a man is said to be "objective" if he "considers all the facts," is "impersonal," "subjects his judgment to public confirmation," and so on, so that finally "objectivity" seems almost synonymous with justice and truth and among the highest human ideals. But is it so? Our question concerns the famous distinction between objective and subjective truth first discerned by Kierkegaard.

The English word "truth" is derived from the Anglo-Saxon "troth," which is still in use in its own right. Truth in this original sense is a form of *fidelity*: fidelity in action, as when friends are true or faithful to one another; fidelity in speech, as when a man truly or faithfully reports what he has seen to another, or is faithful or true to what he has promised another. Truth is therefore originally personal trustworthiness;

we can believe true men and believe in true witnesses. Its original opposite is a *lie*. *Derived* from the lie is a secondary contrast of "incorrect" judgment. The difference between a lie and an error can be used to make clear a general difference between subjective and objective truth.

An objective judgment is correct when what it says about an object is indeed what the object is. The judgment is one thing, the object another; if they "correspond," then the judgment is "correct." In short, objective correctness is fidelity to the object. The object, for its part, must be something whose nature is independent of the judgment about it; otherwise there could be no correspondence. The thing is what it is, independent of my act of judging it; in its independence of my judgment it is a *public* object, an object whose very independence of my subjective acts resides in its availability to other subjects who may turn their attention to it. The very otherness of objects to me is indeed their openness and availability to others, so that the world of such objects is a public world in principle. Hence any objective judgment I bring to bear on such a domain must in principle *demand* for its verification agreement with other subjective judgments about it. All my judgments about objects require for their verification the agreement of others, an agreement in principle if not in fact. For what I have been trying in the first place to ascertain is precisely that public, hence "objective," character of the object.

There is, then, a strict correlation between the requirement that a judgment about an object be publicly confirmable and the essential character or constitution of the object as such. And this applies, *mutatis mutandis,* to all types of object, perceptual and ideal "mathematical" objects alike; as objects, they are all independent of my private subjective experiences, and hence available to others as identical points of reference. To

be an object is to be something to which plural subjective
experiences can direct themselves—plural acts of consciousness,
a single identity of object. And so for all the objective properties of the object. Here "true" means necessarily "true for
all." Its contrary is that which is true for me alone. Objectively considered, what is true for me alone is an *error;* the
object is not what I think it is, and my judgment, instead of
expressing the object's nature, expresses only my own. I have
lost veridical rapport with the objective world, live in a world
of fantasy, caprice, delusion. I have erred or wandered from
the world of objectivity. In this vein Heraclitus: "At night
each lives in his own world; in the day, all live in the same
world." Subjectivity here is the night world, measured objectively against the "same" objective world.

And unquestionably there is a massive value to objective
truth; but just as unquestionably, it is not so massive as to
exclude its subjective contrary. Michael Polanyi has argued
persuasively [3] that even this ideal picture of scientific objectivity is false; not merely are impersonal truth and impersonal
verification impossible in fact, they are also impossible in
principle. But even so, there is a radical contrast between
scientific truth, no matter how qualified, and subjective truth.
This difference may be measured by the difference between a
lie and an error, between witnessing and observing, between
fidelity to oneself and others and fidelity of objective description. The former in each case describes a subjective truth, the
latter objective correctness. How indeed can one be "faithful"
to *objects* except by a feeble metaphorical translation? Is not
one's fidelity to objects really a fidelity to others and oneself
about objects? One can be true only to persons; to objects one

[3] Michael Polanyi, *Personal Knowledge: Towards a Post-Critical Philosophy* (Chicago: University of Chicago Press, 1958).

can only be attentive, with the hope that one's judgments about them will be correct.

Is there some domain of being where there could be no question of objective truth, of truth "about," of "interpersonal verification"; a domain characterized essentially by non-objectivity, by truth "to," and by the need not for interpersonal verification but for the personal honor of a witness? But this domain has already been indicated: the subjective, as it is for itself. It is not an object to itself, and its relation to itself is not aimed at an independent objectivity or the accumulation of correct judgments about itself, but is rather an affair of honor. Here consciousness is its own unique witness, which neither requires nor permits intersubjective verification. Reflexivity is a form of self-witness in which the reflection and the reflected upon are one and the same ego, yet in which the inherent freedom of the witness permits that falsification called hypocrisy, or lying to oneself. This particular act of subjectivity is indeed an ontological modification of the self and not the formation of externally incorrect opinions about oneself; in *this* domain, falsehood makes a difference both to the liar and to the lied about, since they are one and the same. Subjective truth and lies are *constitutive* of subjective being; they are not "about" anything. Further, consciousness as the witness of itself cannot be modified by any objective facts or by any interpersonal tests. Here the truth of the witness is effected and known only by the witness; if he lies, there can be no outside help. It would be a poor madman indeed who could not provide himself with sufficient justification for his delusion.

If the objective sense of truth as correctness or fidelity to some independent object seems primary, it does so only when we ignore the fact that we can have no fidelities to objects but

only to ourselves and other persons, and that in both cases
the relationship is purely internal, fidelity to each singular
self and finally to the dual "we" of love. The primacy of subjective truth over objective correctness therefore rests ontologically on the impossibility of an independently existing external
relationship of correspondence or correctness; these external
relations between judgments and objects must be enacted
somewhere, and where else but in that which can be related
to itself, internally, and what is that but the subjective self
itself? Hence the ontological *ground* even of objective truth
is that subject which can be true to or faithful to itself and
others.

Finally, it is commonly thought that only the universal and
objective can be expressed and communicated. Now it may be
true that *verbal* expression or communication always requires
universal meanings, since words acquire their sense through
rules, and universal rules that give them meaning may therefore be presupposed. But of course it hardly follows from this
circumstance that what the words communicate is nothing but
the universal rules for their own application. Hence if I say,
"I love you," these sounds would have no meaning at all to
another person unless he implicitly grasped their general meaning; and yet what the sentence expresses is nothing universal
at all, but rather the confession of one singular being to another, denoted by "I" and "you." Now one might agree but
add: All that such a sentence *expresses* of the singular is that
which is general, a relationship of "loving," which is "exemplified" in this singular instance. The opening pages of
Hegel's *Phenomenology of Mind* argue that what we now
call the "egocentric particulars"—this, here, now, I—express
nothing about the singulars they denote beyond what is universal in them; and therefore their initial denotative function
is immediately raised *(aufgehoben)* to the universal. But this

neat demonstration does not have the purpose of eliminating their denotative function altogether, but merely that of showing that that function is inseparable from general meaning. It was Bertrand Russell who thought the egocentric particulars could be eliminated altogether, but those arguments have recently been elegantly disposed of.[4]

Further, communication is hardly exhausted in verbal communication; what are we to say of gestures, facial expressions, and indeed the whole visible expressive life of the body? And while all these forms of expression may illustrate general rules, it is surely not true that they communicate only through a prior understanding of those rules. For the rules they are supposed to illustrate have yet to be worked out even by those who believe in them, while the gestures continue to be as perfectly expressive as ever. Meanwhile it remains doubtful that the expressiveness of anything like the gestures and life of the body in its world ever could be reducible to formulable rules. A few conventional acts like shaking hands offer the most plausible bases for the notion that gestures are intelligible only through rules; but the notion seems hopelessly artificial when we consider other ways of learning meanings, such as imitation and empathy, which have nothing whatsoever to do with rules of gesture that must first be learned and then applied in specific cases. Surely we must abandon the prejudice we cherish as speaking animals that only speech is meaningful, and that singular acts themselves have meaning only to the extent that they can be talked about or comprehended in terms of abstract general rules; and the prejudice of generalizing minds that since some things act in accordance with general rules, they act regularly *because of* the rules or because of a *knowledge* of the rules.

[4] Asher Moore, *The Center of the World*, Boston Studies in the Philosophy of Science, III (Dordrecht, Netherlands: D. Reidel), 1967, 356–75.

The essential function of egocentric particulars is to denote the singular; this function can be performed only by the actual use of the term. The "I" in the dictionary is only the "I" of general rules of usage; but it denotes *me* only when I actually speak it. To denote a singular existence requires an act in existence; otherwise we have only the general rule. The terms "I" and "you," then, can be denotative only in their actual use by an existent speaker to an existent hearer. Their denotative meanings are *inseparable* from the singular persons speaking and hearing them. Their meanings are not objective, but essentially bound up with the subjective existence of the persons speaking and hearing them. Communication that inherently implies the existence of one who speaks and another who is spoken to we shall call "subjective" communication, in contrast to "objective" communication, in which a certain impersonal content first present before one mind is transferred to another more or less intact, since both its first and second mental sites are irrelevant to that content. Objective communication is inherently impersonal, subjective communication inherently personal. And since objective communication is inherently independent of the existences of speaker and hearer, its content is inherently irrelevant to those existences. Neither existence need be implied in that content in order for it to be understood. Whether *in addition* the speaker and hearer wish to take some attitude toward it is up to them, but it is not necessary for their comprehension of the content.

Analogously, performatory expressions such as "I promise" essentially imply subjective existence, since the very sense of the expression is the performance of an act; and while the act may illustrate a general rule, it is not itself a general rule or an objective content, but the very act in existence itself.

In sum, intelligible verbal expression may require the comprehension of general rules governing the language to be intelligible, but it is hardly limited to the expression of general rules, concepts, or universals. And intelligible expression is not limited to verbal expression. The living body itself could hardly be more expressive; and surely the whole panorama of the arts, and not literature alone, raises expression to its highest degree. At this point only enough has been said about expression and communication to show that the subjective, the singular, and the existent are all quite capable of being expressed and communicated in language that employs general rules, and that they hardly require even language to be expressive themselves. But we shall return to this theme later.

Philosophy and Explanation

There has always been a degenerative tendency in philosophy to ape the mathematical or natural sciences. In its preoccupation with the universal, it begins to take on the character of a system of logic or mathematics, and thereby turns the singular, existent, and historical into the illustrative; in its preoccupation with the objective, the not-me, it looks like some generalized natural science, confined by the methods of experiment, observation, and hypothesis and either resting on the latest results of the science or contenting itself with common sense. In either case it turns the subjective into the inaccessible and irrelevant. The net result is that each ego, as it is for itself firstpersonally, becomes invisible to philosophy; that ego is not a universal, nor is its singular historical life irrelevant to it, nor is it subject to public observation and experiment like an object, nor is its own singular life characterizable for it only through "hypotheses."

But the matter is worse than this. For neither science nor philosophy aping science wishes simply to describe things. The ideal aim, of course, is always *to explain*. Explanation ideally explains something when it shows how it could not have been otherwise; it could not have been otherwise because of those other objective events upon which it depends for its occurrence, its "causes" or "conditions." *Why* is this water boiling? If it is water, and if water is a "liquid" of such-and-such a sort, and if the perceptible flame beneath it is a "rapid oxidation," and if heat is a "rapid molecular movement," then according to certain thermodynamic laws the "energy" from the one will transfer itself to the other, which will reappear to us as steam.

The perceptible events are first reconceived as "energy systems," the energy systems are related by a law that makes the transfer of energy conceivable through a model, and the resultant explanation is then related back to the perceptible events. These events have now been understood through their conceptual model; they are understood as necessary or perhaps probable, but in either case regular. And thus we make slow progress in finding the causes and conditions of objective events, of understanding how they could not be otherwise. And these explanations give us an undeniable power over the events; to reproduce them we need only assemble the causes, and to alter them we need only alter the causes. It is also clear that explanation through causes is in principle interminable. The causes themselves must have causes, and so no finality is possible. And since anything final or "absolute" could itself have no causes and conditions, it would escape explanation.

If the sciences limit themselves to explaining certain kinds of objects or objective events—astronomical, mechanical, optical, biological, and so on—philosophy now distinguishes itself from the natural sciences by the generality of its field. It will take on the most general phenomena of all—being as such, knowledge as such, value as such—and seek to show how they are possible, or how they could not be otherwise. Both the great rationalistic systems and the probabilistic or empirical philosophies have that in common; if Spinoza wishes to demonstrate the necessity of each objective event in the world, Hume will argue that such a necessity cannot be known, denying necessity in one place in order to reinstall it in the conditions of knowing. Both employ conceptual models to explain the phenomena, Spinoza a model of Nature as such, Hume a model of human nature. Philosophy for both is explanation: for Spinoza "understanding the place of mind in Nature," for Hume understanding the place of the idea of nature in the human mind.

Now unquestionably these systematic philosophical attempts to grasp the necessity for the most general features of the world are dazzling intellectual spectacles. At the same time, it may be worth inquiring whether philosophy so conceived could possibly lead to anything we might reasonably call wisdom. Explanatory philosophy hopes to understand the necessity of the most general features of the world or of our experience of it or our action in it. But the contemplation of necessity is not the illumination of what is not necessary or general or objective, namely, the domain of life as it is lived first-personally. Whatever necessities that domain also illustrates, it is not in the realm of the necessary that choices are made and the existential-contingent encountered. The injunction "Know thyself" is not an invitation to find an explanation of yourself, as though one were to psychoanalyze oneself. And yet it does demand knowledge and forbid folly; and so the kind of knowledge for which it asks must be different from any form of objective explanation. It is this other form of knowledge or illumination we shall try to circumscribe here, the illumination or clarification of life as it is lived, a project close to Karl Jaspers' *Existenzerhellung*.

Even the first glance at the domain of life, taken autobiographically, is sufficient to show that it could be illuminated only by radically different categories from those appropriate to the objective not-me. And finally we shall have to conclude that it is not illuminated by any categories at all. But let us leave that for the conclusion; there is a preliminary categorical demarcation of a domain where the decisive and essential thing is the irrelevance of all categorical description. But even that requires the preliminary work of circumscription.

In the present instance, whatever understanding we have of our own lives is not based on any explanation of them. My acts proceed from my decisions; my decisions are and are known by me to be *mine*. That is, my acts originate in my decisions; if that is their origin, they are not further explainable as being caused by some objective not-me. They are therefore not further explainable by causes, but arise out of those free decisions. And yet they are not therefore unintelligible to me; they are what I understand best. But I understand them in a way categorically different from that of understanding by causal explanation. The truth is that if these acts and decisions were caused by something objective and independent of me, they would necessarily lose whatever sense they might have for me. Every effort to see any life as the product of objective causes independent of that life must necessarily find that life senseless to itself. If someone should object that my decision was, after all, made with respect to a situation external to me or it would have been senseless, we have only to notice that any choice is made only in regard to a situation that appears alterable by the action of the one who chooses; it is with respect to my possible action that a situation can be said to exist at all. It is therefore the possibility of my free action that discloses the nature of a situation; and what is disclosed is possibilities and alternatives. My possibility of action therefore opens up the world in which I am as a set of possibilities, and my action is my free response to those possibilities. My action is therefore not caused by the situation, nor is the situation itself objectively definable independent of my own subjective freedom. My decision, then, is not objectively explainable by my situation.

If I am asked to "explain" my decisions, I am certainly not being asked to give causes for them, but to express their purpose or sense. And so we are at once in an ontological domain that demands its own terms, whose meanings are unique to that domain. If subjective decision is an origin, objectively we can discover no origins, but only the interminability of causes and conditions. If subjectively we shall discover something final and absolute, there is no finality or anything absolute objectively. If subjectively we can discover sense, purpose, and meaning, objectively these terms have no application at all. Explanation, then, as a process of showing the development of events in accordance with a law that requires them to develop in a certain way and no other, introduces into the domain of subjectivity a form of thought wholly irrelevant and inappropriate to it. Insofar as philosophy seeks this sort of explanation, it necessarily excludes that autobiographical and subjective domain where we all are and must be, willy-nilly. Of course, all this was clearly said by Socrates in the *Crito*. Mechanical explanations would have carried his bones out of prison at once; yet all he sought was the "good."

Ontological Autobiography

In its pursuit of a universally valid, objective explanation of things in general, philosophy has frequently turned its vision so far outward that even when it has reached the threshold of success, it has done so at the cost of losing its initial ideal, the love of wisdom. By forgetting what Socrates seems never to have forgotten, that philosophy must direct its efforts toward that knowing which is of its own nature essential to the knower and constitutive of his existence, so that its absence is not merely ignorance about something but a foolish life, philosophy has indeed chased down the answers to curious problems, but it remains questionable to what extent the answers fall within the domain of that which it is essential to know.

"Know thyself" requires of us one thing: that each know *who he is.* We know who we are preliminarily when we know where we have been, where we are, and where we can go. But at any given moment this is nothing other than the most lucid autobiographical consciousness we can attain. To locate wisdom in the domain of the autobiographical might seem at first glance to be its most profound dislocation. Is not wisdom the discovery that I am a nullity? And if it is not that, is it not an invitation to narcissism, egotism, and self-inflation, or to their opposite, self-denunciation? Would it not lead to an obsession with the past? And why should anyone else be interested? Moreover, has anyone the slightest hope of success? Why call it ontological or even philosophical when it is nothing but personal excavation and confession? In the end, to burden a reader with such matters might look like the perfection of tactlessness.

And yet if my life is what I have done and what I have suffered, it clearly cannot be *about me,* as if I were its exclusive theme. My actions and responses are actions and responses in my world, a world far from being populated by myself alone; if it were, both action and response would be impossible. As for the narcissism of my reflections upon my life, what reason could be given for the implied assumption that I must judge myself, either well or ill, or submit myself to the moral judgments of others? Is there no possibility of thought sufficiently lucid to preclude moral judgment? And if autobiography usually is indeed retrospective, that may lie in the circumstance that it is not ontological, that it has not pushed its reflections far enough to uncover the sort of being it is that *can have* an autobiography, namely, a self with a past but also a present and a presumptive future. My consciousness of my life would certainly include also my consciousness of where I now am and where I can go. It could be imprisoned in its own past only if it had no present or future—that is, after death. Why should anyone else be interested? If the "why" asks for some universally compelling reason that would oblige all other human beings to be interested in *my* autobiography, such a reason certainly could not be found. But we might consider two related matters: If no reasons can be found to explain why anyone should be interested in anyone else, we have in one stroke dissolved love and society; and if no one took any interest in his own life, we would in one stroke have dissolved personal responsibility and personality itself into precisely the mindless folly warned against by the oracle. To hope for some success in this domain is not to boast of having attained it; but without the hope there would only be the certainty of failure. And as for wisdom being the discovery that one is at last nothing—nothing before God, nothing to nature, nobody to one's fellows, and finally of no importance to oneself—such a sequence of annihilating judgments can surely be freely made, but we are hardly compelled by either logic, phenomenology, or wisdom to repeat them. If life is a nullity, it is so only because it has freely chosen so to be; other free choices are possible.

Human life as it is for the man living it and not as it is apprehended by others, or as it is supposed to arise from inferred physical causes or hidden psychological forces, is reflected in consciousness. It is therefore in principle accessible to that consciousness through reflection. What exists in consciousness can be reflectively known by that very same consciousness. Human existence, then, is autophenomenal: it shows itself to the very subjectivity living it. But, as everyone knows, it can also be masked, concealed, or distorted. If consciousness is inherently true, it is so only "in principle"; in fact, it perpetually retains the power and desire to conceal itself from itself. It is also the great liar, not chiefly to others, but to itself. If consciousness were not a liar, it would have no problems, particularly that of self-lucidity. And if consciousness were not lucidity itself—that is, truth—it could not lie to itself, since it would not be aware of what it had to lie about; it could not be foolish but only ignorant. And so the problem lies in the perplexing realm of lies and in the task of clearing out as many as may be desirable. And while help from all quarters is acceptable, the final assessor of truth must remain the reflexive subjectivity itself. This final assessment can cover only that truth which I conceal from myself; it therefore is only accidentally concerned with such objective facts as the date of my birth but is essentially concerned with uncovering for me who I am. There could be no higher authority on that question than myself, beyond which I cannot in principle go. My ultimate assessment of who I am, where I have been, and where I can go is not—again in principle—subject to another authority; for it remains I who must accredit that other and test his hypotheses against my own reflective and intuitive acquaintance with myself. This is evidently true even for psychoanalysts, who cannot impose their own interpretations on patients who do not accept the validity of those interpretations.

To whatever extent we can know ourselves, we have gathered together in reflection where we have been, where we are, and where we can go. We have excavated ourselves from the massive and delusive image we have ourselves forged from objective opinions and public or scientific laws, and have done so with truth. But such an autobiographical consciousness must not be considered as simply a mirror reflection, an accompanying image of a life that could just as easily have run along its own course without it. For obviously it is only if I know who and where I am without deception that I can act and respond without deception. The autobiographical consciousness, then, is the solitary basis for honest existence, for choice and decision, and for the disclosure of genuine alternatives in the future. It is therefore that knowledge which is essential to the knower to know, and not a system of correct opinions about an objective domain where I have nothing to do or say.

Human life is thus a unique form of being; it is so generically, there being nothing else quite like it. But what is indicated even by the generic form "human life" is that the essential thing is not at all the generic but always the unique, singular, unrepeatable, the historical and autobiographical. No *general* ontology can possibly succeed in its aim if it does not consider and make room for this unique form of being, a form of being in which the singular is essential. And it cannot help missing its goal if it does not look at singular life as that life appears to the subjectivity living it, autobiographically. But if the essential in human life is necessarily the unrepeatable and singular, there can be no possibility of any *general* ontology at all. In its generality, it would necessarily have to miss the very essence of one form of being, human being.

Philosophy as Phenomenology

If we have before our eyes a distinctive realm of being (each man's life), and if that realm is considered from a certain point of view (as it is for himself) and with a certain purpose (understanding it), we have isolated a domain that is subjective and not objective, in which the singular takes precedence over the universal, and in which there is no question of explaining but only of a responsive understanding: in a word, our own singular and unrepeatable destinies as they are for ourselves and one another. Since all of this is, it constitutes a domain of ontology; and since it is and must be of primary concern to ourselves and indeed supplies the foundation for any so-called objective knowledge, it consigns all other modes of knowledge to the secondary and derived. Not only is it primordial itself, but it must equally well be a primordial interest of anything that seeks to be more general. And since it has its own unique form of expression and communication— its own methods, as it were—those methods must take precedence logically over all others.

The method already formulated which usually offers itself as a candidate for our interest here is that of phenomenology. And indeed this method is so close to my own that only the most careful inquiry can disclose where the utility of phenomenology lies and where it too must finally collapse into autobiographical confession. I am thinking now exclusively of Edmund Husserl's phenomenology, and not of the innumerable versions of it by those who, in attempting to follow him, made radical modifications in his method. Phenomenology too locates its standpoint in the ego; everything must be clarified as it is for the ego; no hypotheses about what things *must* be like, about that which cannot be meaningful for the ego, can be admitted. The world and the ego itself are what they are for the ego, and nothing else. So far, so good; this fundamental viewpoint, which disregards all naturalistic, metaphysical, and logical assumptions derived from elsewhere and from other premises, coincides with my own. I do not say there *is* nothing else; I only eliminate everything else from my concern. I shall accordingly consider my life only insofar as it can be autophenomenal, insofar as I can be conscious of it, and not to the extent that I cannot be conscious of it.

"Can" and "cannot" are, of course, matters of principle, not of practice; we know only what can be made clear by the accomplishment of its clarification, and that is an affair of practice. In effect, then, the methodological principle of reducing human existence to what it shows itself to be excludes nothing in practice, nor does it assign any factual limits to investigation; it has only a theoretical import in relation to other theories; its practical import is a renewed invitation to return to those mysterious phenomena themselves as they present themselves to us. Let us first try to see what these phenomena are, before we lose ourselves in theoretical constructions that assume that the phenomenon of life is itself obvious. That it is not obvious should itself be obvious; further reflection will penetrate to the very limits of what lies hidden in the obvious. The *initial* standpoint of phenomenology, then, is identical with mine.

But Husserl's phenomenology had other aims and goals. The chief of these was insight into the transcendental *structuring* done by the ego in order to constitute its world. Phenomenology here aims at a "rigorous science" of certain synthetic a priori "essences" enacted by "the" ego, in order to give a universal sense to what it would call "world." And so, accordingly, we have Husserl's detailed analyses of the essence of perception, the essence of ideation, and the essence of the constitution of ideal significances, existent things, and other subjectivities. They aimed at *insight*. But insight, strictly considered, can be had only into necessary or essential connections; there can be no insight into the accidental, except that it is indeed accidental—that is, not necessary. And so Husserl aimed at a vast transcendental map of essential and necessary connections, within which the ego could catch itself at work constituting necessarily now this and now that. The pattern of its work was already inscribed on the map; the accidental facts of its life were not, and were of no interest to "strict science." They were at the start disregarded.

For all the distinctiveness of this approach, its aims were not far distant from those of Plato or of Kant: the effort to understand the *a priori* eternal connections that existent persons only enact, and which they must know on pain of being ignorant or naive. With Husserl the aspiration to a universal science of consciousness and its object is explicit; the *factual* is disregarded at the start as accidental to the essential; the factual is what *could* be otherwise, and thus is of no interest to phenomenology, which looks for what could not be otherwise. The factual is but an erasable blackboard diagram for a mathematician looking at the ideal meaning exemplified by it. And yet that erasable mark is what represents each human existence in its contingency. And so while the accidental *facts* of birth and death have an ideal absurdity and can easily be disregarded by the phenomenologists, their meanings as "birth" and "death" *are* phenomenologically and ideally clarifiable, and thus are included among the phenomenologist's concerns. Yet neither the meaning "death" nor the meaning "birth" is the subjective or existential concern of existing men; it is the fact itself. While indeed every fact must exemplify some ideal essence or be absolutely meaningless, it is not that ideal meaning which *concerns* existent subjects so much as the *fact* that exemplifies it. Our own autobiographical interests concern precisely that which Husserl's phenomenology eliminated from its concern at the start: radical contingency, the accidental, the *fact,* which cannot be deduced from anything.

Accordingly, Husserl was concerned only with the essential

connections between ideal meanings and the ego. For him this ego was at one and the same time the individual self and the transcendental self; his analysis moves toward a pluralistic monadology of transcendental subjects. I am both a transcendental ego and myself as "empirical" or "psychological" ego. And yet the aspect of the transcendental ego that alone concerned Husserl was its universal character; it is always "the" ego, the ego insofar as it exhibited a universal function, namely, that of constituting an interpersonal world. Toward the end Husserl even attempted to clarify the structures of its *development* through a "genetic" phenomenology; but as always, his phenomenology aimed at the principles and essence of such development, not at its actual history with all its accidents and contingencies and possibilities of free choice, which are the stuff of history and autobiography both.

Since what I am here seeking to demarcate is a domain of being, human being as it is for itself, I shall view the realm of being from the phenomenological standpoint, but for purposes quite different from Husserl's. Since I wish to demarcate a domain of being where the *accidental is essential,* and since that domain is that of human existence as it is first-personally or autobiographically, the demarcation itself takes place on phenomenological grounds; my argument will therefore be fundamentally *negative,* to the effect that human beings must necessarily escape any "eidetic" or "essential" analysis; in effect, that there can be no "theory" of human life, no "essence" to it, and no "insight" into it. But these contentions are themselves of a theoretical order. And so I shall use phenomenological methods to demonstrate their own limits; what lies beyond the limits is human life itself, whose proper record and expression is each man's autobiography. This essay is not that autobiography, but the demarcation of its domain on theoretical grounds. Phenomenology will always say something essential to my topic; but how and where it is and is not essential can be clarified only by its radical contrast, ontological autobiography.

Two Sides of Consciousness

Phenomenology employs two terms that are useful to my argument: "intentionality" and "reflexivity."

Intentionality, of course, has been widely studied by phenomenologists, and here I shall repeat only certain relevant features of it. That any conscious act is related to something that is not itself and which forms its object, content, or meaning hardly seems to require elaborate argument. But what should be carefully borne in mind is that there are many modes of intentionality, and not only the one that is the favorite of philosophers, cognition, whether perceptual or conceptual. Rather grave errors emerge from the effort to make all modes of consciousness analogous to cognition, as though, for example, to fear something were the same as simply to "know" it as fearful. Common speech discriminates a great many kinds of consciousness: perception, imagination, memory, anticipation, dreaming, feeling, desiring, willing, conceiving, and so on. And each of these in turn represents a cluster of related types of consciousness. Within what we call "memory" we might easily distinguish recall, reminiscence, recollection, retention, and so on. All of these kinds of consciousness are kinds of intentionality. Each kind of intentionality intends its own *appropriate* object in its own way. Hence just as the visible cannot be an object for hearing or the audible for seeing, the past is not an object for perception and the present is not an object for memory. Each mode of intentionality intends its object in its own unique way and intends its own unique object. There is, then, a strict correlation between the intentional act and the intended object. To see an apple is not the same as to desire it; and for its part the apple as intentional object shows different faces to these different intentionalities. To vision the apple is a sphere; to touch, hard; to appetite, luscious. I can touch the thing I see; but I cannot touch color or see hardness. Correspondingly, to *will* an action is to intend that act as "something to be done," and not simply cognitively to entertain it as a pure possibility. To fear a reptile is not simply to see it or to pose it as an object before the mind, but to fear it as fearful. Its fearfulness can originally be given only to fear. After its original disclosure, it can then secondarily become a theme of other intentionalities.

Not only do objects disclose their appropriate *properties* to the appropriate intentionality, but their disclosed *ontological status* also is correlative to the original mode of intentional disclosure. The past as such is disclosed originally only to retention or memory; present existence is given originally only to perception; the future originally only to anticipation; the possibly existent originally only to imagination; the eternal originally only to reason. And these are only a few of the more conspicuous modalities of being, which can be modulated in an infinite variety of ways.

To find that consciousness is invariably related intentionally to an object or class of objects does not in the least dictate that those "objects" must be *existent*. Obviously, they can have whatever ontological status they do have; my present intentionality can relate itself, for example, to what is nonexistent— to the past or future or imaginary or possible. All of these types of being can have their own peculiar effectivity for me without actually being existent. When I plan today to do something tomorrow, that tomorrow, precisely in its character as future and not yet, effectively determines my present consciousness and activity.

If any act of consciousness is related to its object through *intentionality,* it is related to *itself* by *reflexivity.* And yet it is doubtful if the term "related" could be anything but ambiguous in this connection, an invitation to perpetual confusions, misleading analogies, and misguided refutations. The term "relation" inherently suggests two or more things, distinct in themselves, between which an external connection has been established by the act of relating them. But here the *primordially* reflexive thing is the subject I; and if anything whatsoever is clear, it is that the ego is one and not two subjects brought into relationship by an external connection. The primary fact is always that *I am I,* and it is this unique fact that we characterize as "reflexivity." I am I, and I *know* I am I, and I do *not* know it by inference, from reports given to me by others, or simply as an example of a universally valid logical principle of identity. I know it directly, and this direct self-acquaintance is identical with the self. I am not a committee of selves, each looking at the other in an endeavor to ascertain whether that other is *really* itself. Nor is reflexivity itself a particularly apt term if it is understood as one of those mirror reflections that perpetually mislead Sartre. For if I look at myself in the mirror, I have no *direct* assurance that it is I who is being reflected; perhaps originally I had to move a part of my body and note the parallelism between it and its image until finally I could trust the image alone. But how could any of these conditions be duplicated within the ego itself? I am fundamentally an identity, a self, and not something or other reduplicated in a reflection, shadow, or echo.

The truth seems to be rather that the ego, I, or self cannot be characterized at all in terms appropriate for objects. Objects and their objective world offer themselves as characterizable external relations, properties, qualities, locations, causalities, and the rest of the common categories; but none of these categories seems appropriate to the self, and if one of them is to be used, it must be regarded as a radically inappropriate metaphor, useful only to indicate something it does not literally describe. The method of refuting any characterization of the ego is therefore easy and sketched out in advance. All that an ego need do to refute a characterization of itself is to take *anything objectively said* about itself literally; it will then fail to find itself to be as it has been described. Rather than play this clever but futile game, it would seem wiser to note the dangers of any literal description in objective terms, and, for the valid *sense* of what is said, revert phenomenologically to the primordial *experience* the self has of itself: self-presence.

The problem, which I believe is inherent to the situation, might suggest to some that there is some mystery or difficulty about the nature of the self. But if anything is true, it is that the self is *not* problematical, questionable, or mysterious to it-self; it becomes problematical only to the extent that it en-deavors to deny its own self-acquaintance, turn itself inside out, and look for itself as though it were one more object in the objective world, a peculiar kind of object that some "authori-ties" think exists while others do not. If instead we relocate our philosophical position where it must inherently be anyway, in ourselves *not* dissociated from ourselves, the situation is reversed; it is not the self that is problematical to itself, but rather *the whole objective world*. The self in principle is wholly and completely transparent to itself. It lives, so to speak, in its own light, a light that illumines various opacities in the objective world. The self is *exhaustively* autophenom-enal to itself in principle.

The entire problem of description, then, is comprehensible

in its origins, and analogies can easily be found elsewhere. For radically different modes of being, it is hardly surprising that categories suitable for one may be incommensurate with others. Value becomes a mystery to languages of fact, organisms to languages of mechanism, and anything genuinely infinite or absolute to languages of the finite and relative. And since the objective was originally characterized by its otherness to subjectivity, it is not surprising that the very essence of subjectivity resides in its inability to be characterized in any literal sense by the use of categories appropriate to that other, objective world. But ordinary language is not so impoverished as to be limited to objectivity; the ordinary language of subjectivity, while not reducible to that of objectivity, is nevertheless rich enough for most purposes. And so we already have a vocabulary appropriate enough to its own sphere. In the literature of subjectivity characteristic terms are freedom rather than causation; intention rather than literal direction; the reflexive rather than the simple or immediate; meanings rather than causes; values rather than facts; negation rather than affirmation; and finally truth as honesty rather than as propositional correctness. We shall be exploring these matters in greater detail in a moment. Meanwhile we can observe the precaution of securing the sense of subjective terms not by objectively thinking about what they designate, but by reoccupying the reflexive standpoint and reanimating their sense by reenacting what they invite. Subjectivity proper is always lived, not objectively thought about, looked at, or "posed" in any fashion whatsoever before the mind. It is not primarily *before* itself at all, but reflexively bound up with itself in the form of immediate self-awareness. To put myself before myself in the form of an image or concept is to effect nothing less than an internal dissociation; and while some such thing is possible, there is no need to suppose that it is necessary or "philosophical" or anything but the worst way conceivable of understanding my-self. For while consciousness can grasp something of itself in this embarrassed, self-alienated, dissociated form, it can hardly understand that which has become self-alienated through this process; on the other hand, self-alienation can easily be understood as a product of decomposition of the authentic ego.

These somewhat abstract considerations serve only to estab-lish a point of view and a vocabulary with which we can even-tually return to our chief theme, ontological autobiography. But perhaps they are sufficient to indicate that if wisdom inherently has something to do with the mind, since it is a form of knowledge, and if in addition wisdom inherently cannot be an abstract, explanatory, or universal grasp of ob-jectivities external to the mind that searches for it, then per-haps a *reflexive* or subjective recuperation of the mind from its absorption in the objective may enable us to locate its domain with more precision. In short, "Know thyself" can hardly be a command to acquire objective propositions about oneself, a sort of self-psychology, whether those propositions be true or false, but must point to another mode of conscious-ness altogether, so far roughly limned as enacted reflexivity. Reflexivity presents some opportunity to define that form of knowing which is *identical with being;* and where should that be found except in that being whose essence is knowing—provided, of course, that the "knowing" in question is not objective intentionality, a "knowing about things," even when one of those "things" looks something like myself?

One final remark: If the intentional aspect of conscious-ness relates the ego to some objectivity in some definite mode, such as perception or desire, and if primary reflexivity relates the ego to itself, then, since the ego is an identity, any of its intentional acts, simple in themselves, may by the effect of reflexivity become reflexive. Thus desire, in itself a simple act directed toward the desired, may be modified by reflexivity into the desire to desire, or the affirmation of desire, which is will. Perception can become deliberate observation, and may eventually be modified into thought. What we aim at in our search for that which it is essential to know, however, is the modification of the infinite varieties of direct intentionalities into reflexive *knowledge*. The emphasis is therefore on the cognitive mode of reflexivity. This choice itself is arbitrary. The ego might equally well choose other aims, terminating in belief, action, poetic expression, or whatever. Those choices, equally arbitrary, would reflect the ontological autobiographies of their authors.

2

The Transcendental Ego

The Method of Divestment

IF I SHOULD listen to the Delphic oracle commanding me to know myself, I could understand it as a task only if I did not know myself already; as Kant's categorical imperative would be senseless to a "holy will," this would be senseless to an angelic spirit. I must then be confused as to who I am and what I am, and my confusion must be a confusion of myself with what I am not. Who or what am I? And should I try to find out by asking this question of the oracle? We would hope the oracle would remain silent, for certainly whatever it was asking for, it was not demanding that we acquire information or correct answers to the problem. What assurance could I have that any answer given back was right? In short, while I am now confused as to who I am, I must also have all the resources available for a solution, as well as the criteria at hand for conviction. In the long run, it will be myself I must satisfy and not the oracle. And so our entire task must be understood as self-explication. If I am to come to know myself, I must first distinguish myself from what I am not; and who is to be the judge of what I am and what I am not except me? Perhaps this is all I am.

Let us take the term "I" at first as a pure index, pointing to myself in whatever form or shape I may eventually disclose myself to be. I shall therefore try to ignore any prior connotations or characterizations that may lurk around the term. It is precisely that "characterization" I am looking for. My position is that of confusion; that is, I am for myself confused with what I am not. The initial step of the task is therefore clear: to divest myself of all that I am not. But the I that is taking this step is a *conscious* self. Hence the divestment itself will be an act of consciousness, and this act of consciousness will discriminate what is me from what is not me. We need have no misgivings that to discriminate the pure self from the world would require a factual removal from the world, or death. Nothing of the sort is required, of course, any more than the discrimination of the shape of something from its color requires that the thing be dismembered into two separate things, a shapeless color and a colorless shape.

If now I reflect that anything that I could possibly perceive or apprehend as an object in any way whatsoever—in memory, in anticipation, or by abstract thought, for example—is necessarily apprehended as not me, I can easily enough take the first step and apprehend reflexively that in my present, first-person-singular aspect, I am not and cannot be an object for me; no object I can apprehend can be me. I am therefore absolutely nonobjective; and if the "world" is taken as an "objective world," or a world of things and events that are objective, I can never be a member of that world.

If it should be objected that while for *myself* I am not one more object or member of a domain of objects, for another I the objective world may nevertheless be such an object or have an objective aspect, the answer must lie in the further consideration that what I am for myself has an absolute priority over what I am for another. For if the other apprehends me as a self objective to him, what he is indeed apprehending is that I, in my subjective aspect for myself, am also an objective other to him; but precisely what is it that is objective to him unless it is myself in my subjectivity? In other words, if he indeed apprehends me, then he must be apprehending what I am for myself. Hence what I am is what I primordially apprehend myself to be. And though at the same time I may be indirectly apprehended as an object by someone else, my possible objectification to another can have no effect on my own first-personal subjectivity. My subjectivity therefore underlies any derived objectification, and remains logically and ontologically prior to any of its derived appearances or modes.

This is true even when I objectify myself; that is, when I "think about" myself, "look at myself," or introspectively try to form an "image" of myself. Such mental acts are certainly possible and often are even confused with reflexivity; but what infects them all is again the fundamental condition of objectivity: to be an object is to be other to the subject for whom the object is an object. If therefore I pose myself to myself as an objective theme, I am simply apprehending myself under those conditions that transform me into an other; hence I achieve objectivity only at the cost of losing my primary awareness of myself as myself. In a word, any thematic posing of myself before myself, any objectification whatsoever, is but an expression of the possibility in any self of being alienated from itself; and self-alienation can hardly be pri-

mary, since it presupposes that there is a self that *can* be
self-alienated. Hence if we desire to follow the Delphic oracle,
it is obviously useless to ask *it* what we are or to attempt to
form some objective picture of ourselves, to see ourselves as
others see us, or to form images of ourselves as actors on a
stage, whom we might also see from the audience. As I remarked in the previous chapter, intentionality names the relationship of my consciousness to what is other; reflexivity
names the relationship in consciousness of myself to myself.
Hence no intentional act of consciousness of mine can primarily grasp me as I am for myself; that grasp remains reflexive and immediate. What reflexivity grasps is a self that
can divest itself of the entire domain of the objective.

The next stage of divestment, the divestment of all universality, looks even more fatal to any hopes we may have
entertained for knowledge and communication, but in fact it
is not. I am a self; that is, a reflexive identity, a singularity.
The self is precisely that sort of being to whom singularity is
essential; in other words, to say "singular," "reflexive," and
"self" is to say precisely the same thing three ways. Nothing
but a self can inherently be self-identical. Other objects may
be "identical" for a self, but they are not identical in themselves; they simply are. Identity, as Hegel has shown, is itself
a reflexive relationship. To be an identity is to be identical-to-
self; that is, a self. The sole kind of being that can *be* in the
mode of an internal reflex is consciousness; hence it is not by
accident that identities first and last are egos. To be a self-
identical or reflexive singular, then, is to be an ego or self, and
that is inherently and necessarily a singular, just me and just
you. There is therefore no abstractly universal self or general
self. To be a self is not to be an instance of "selfhood,"
"egoity," or any other supposed universal; it is to be just me
and just you in our irreplaceable singularities. There is no

universal that characterizes these singular selves, for any such universal must, simply because it is universal, omit precisely what it hopes to grasp: the singular self. The universal "self-hood" is no who, no I, and has omitted from selves precisely that which makes them selves.

But, it will be objected, that is exactly what we have been doing here. Hence insofar as we have characterized selves as reflexive singularities, egos, identities, and so on, we have shown that quite the opposite is the case, and that nothing is easier than to characterize selves. They all have something in common, and what they have in common is the abstract character "self-relatedness." But this objection holds only insofar as we do not understand how selves are being characterized. Such definitions as "self-reflexivity," and "conscious identity" are, when analyzed, nothing but negations of the universal, assertions that that which is being so "characterized" has no essential "character" at all, in effect leaving the definition with the double role of canceling out any positive universal essence and functioning as an index for the singular self divested of all universal essence. The term "self" must be grasped absolutely nominalistically. It names the class of beings that are unique in not being essentially characterizable, the beings that instead constitute a class of absolute individuals. I cannot be an instance of the essence "ego," if what is essential to me is my singularity, I myself and *not you;* that singularity cannot be represented in the universal or only represented universally, since its very definition cancels out the universal.

Have we not with this step removed ourselves from the realm of discourse? On the contrary, we make actual discourse possible for the first time. Discourse must be spoken by someone, and the speaker must say "I." It is not *the I* that speaks, but I. "I," however, is an index; it names the speaker without characterizing him and is intelligible only in use. If a man says

"I," everyone knows whom he means; the actual use of the word indicates its sense. Without that actual use, it cannot function as an index; "the speaker" or "speakers as such" can say nothing. When I say "I," I mean me and not you, although you too must say "I." And so while on the surface it looks as though you and I were both instances of "I in general," it is precisely to distinguish me from you that I use "I" in the first place. It is not by accident, therefore, that indices can be "pointers" to singular existence only in the act of being used.

Divestment, then, divests me of all objectivity whatsoever, and at the same time divests my understanding of all categories of objectivity; it divests me of all universality, all essence, all abstract concepts including anything that might look like "concepts" of subjectivity. Divestment must in addition divest me of any final multiplicity, since whatever I am, I am not many me's, a committee or association of selves. If therefore there is any multiplicity in me, it cannot have the implication of infecting me myself with plurality. I must remain that single and singular self that has within him, as if in solution, whatever multiplicity or differentiation can subsequently be discriminated.

The direction of divestment is clear, and there would be no particular purpose served by an effort to name the things I am not: I am not you or he or it, or "selfhood." What am I, then? Obviously, I am I.

The Absolute Ego

"Divestment" is my word for a movement of consciousness that has a long history under other names, such as Descartes's "doubt," in which a "thinking substance" recovers itself with certitude from a whirl of confusion compounded of convictions about an "external world," the deliverances of sense experience, and commonplaces of judgment. Or divestment may be taken as a "purification" of the soul too engrossed with what it is not, too much caught up in that deceptively tempting and deceptively rewarding domain of the impurities of existence, where the poor soul futilely sought itself. Or it is another name for Husserl's "suspension of the natural attitude," an attitude in which the ego naively performs a variety of acts of mind—perception, desire, judgment—without reflecting upon these various acts themselves, thereby condemning itself to a certain blindness about what it itself is. For all their differences, these movements of consciousness have in common a regressive shift of attention from objects or affairs back to the ego that was engrossed with them. This recuperative movement of the ego is not itself just one more engrossment, as though now the ego were to enter into a morbid obsession with itself. The reflexive act by which the ego grasps itself by divesting itself of what it is not is unique and incomparable to any prereflexive act. Further, it is only preliminary to a more general recuperation; the reflexive apperception of the ego by itself would, if taken as the final end of thought, be a remarkably simple and misguided solution to a problem of recuperation that can be enacted only through an entire existence. The ontological autobiography of an ego divested of existence altogether would in effect be no autobiography at all. Nevertheless, no recuperation or solution is even thinkable without it.

And so there may be some value in pausing to examine further some remarkable features of the divested *I am I*. All of these features obtain by virtue of what may be called the "absolute" character of the ego. The ego is a self, and in that capacity it has no internal relationship to any other thing.

Therefore no analysis of the divested ego can disclose in it anything but itself. It is therefore absolute, and internally related to and dependent upon nothing else whatever.

If now we turn our attention to a variety of things that the ego is not, we shall be able to give some sense to terms that characterize, by contrast and negation, the self that is I. Since I discriminate myself as a self in the first place by a radical act of divestment from engrossment in anything other, the first characterization of the transcendental ego is that it is nonexistent. For if existence is taken as a domain of being where something happens, and if the ontological condition for the happening of something is external relatedness, clearly the *I am I* is a dimension where nothing can happen; it is precisely from all happening that I have divested myself. In other words, to exist is to be in a domain where things make a difference to one another, where something can happen to me or where my acts make a difference to others. Existence, then, is the domain of happening, and happening is contingent on the beings to which the happenings happen. Hence no internal analysis of one being in itself can disclose what will happen to it. What happens is an "accident" to it; it is "fortuitous," "contingent on it," "unpredictable" on the basis of either its being alone or the being of the other alone. But in divesting myself of all reference to any other, I have with the same stroke divested myself of existence. And yet I have not divested myself of *being;* I *am* I, and I am not nothing at all, or nonbeing. In divesting myself of existence, then, I clarify the proper mode of being of my ego and disclose at the same time that existence itself is but one mode of being, against which there is at least one other, that of the *I am I.* The "am" in *I am I* names precisely that absolute mode of being in which the singular self, taken by itself, *is.*

If by "temporality" we mean a general character of existence, then it is clear that while I *am,* I am not temporal in this dimension at all. Temporality is the mode of being of passages and events, with their moments of "now," "not yet," "no longer." The moments of temporality, past, present, and future, are essentially interrelated: the past was once present, the future will be present, and the present is neither past nor future, but now. Each moment of temporality, then, receives its position by reference to other moments; nothing in itself can be either past, present, or future. Temporality expresses one general character of existing things, that each exists only in relation to another existing thing, to something that it itself is not. Existence is a domain of finite beings, none of which can exist in itself; temporality, characterizing this domain, necessarily reflects their interrelatedness. If, then, we consider something that is but whose being does not lie in its relationship to anything it is not—namely, the transcendental ego— we have something that is and yet which is not temporal or existent. The mode of being traditionally assigned to anything complete in itself—here the self itself—is "eternity." The divested ego is timeless; it is not in succession to itself, not a process, not a becoming of any sort; in its self-coincidence, it *is* in the preeminent sense of being absolute and eternal.

It might now seem that description of the ego is limited to negative characterizations, so that in the end the very act of divestment by which it recovers itself also divests it of the means by which it might know itself. And yet the true situation is surely the very opposite. For the ego, it is not itself that is obscure and questionable, but rather everything else. It is the domain of the objective or the not-I that is fundamentally opaque, and it is precisely its opacity that enables the objective to be objective to me, a butt for my intentionality. For itself, the ego in its divestment and absoluteness is absolutely transparent, pure "light" itself. It is not the absolute, the eternal, that which is itself that can be characterized by unintelligibility, darkness, or bewilderment; it is only the relative, the existent, that which depends for its being on something else that it is not, that could generate confusion and bewilderment. Hence the divested ego, being eternally coincident with itself in the form of consciousness, finds nothing else within it, nothing behind it or in front of it, nothing out of which it proceeds or into which it passes; in short, it is ontologically an absolute finality. That it can say nothing but *I am I,* looked at in one way, might seem to be the absolute and final impoverishment of its discourse; and indeed it would be if that were the end of the matter. But *I am I* is only the eternal origin of things; it names that which can have an autobiography, and it establishes the character of that which can have anything like a "world" before it and in which it can act. When therefore we next consider the existence of the absolute ego, its life with others in the world, we shall find that its life is at every point a "paradoxical" fusion of the absolute and relative, the eternal and the temporal, the transcendental and the mundane. In a word, experience is through and through metaphysical. It can be so for us since each of us is from the start both absolute and transcendent; it is from the ego itself that metaphysical significances proceed, significances that otherwise might seem "meaningless," "hypothetical," verging on the supernatural if not downright superstitious. We have already noted one such metaphysical meaning, "world"; "ego" itself is another. "World" cannot be given to the ego through any finite experience; its sense is drawn from the absolute ego itself. Nor is ego given to itself through some "inner feeling" or "experience"; its very being is essentially, absolutely, and eternally self-coincident. The only thing that is accidental in this domain is the attention that the ego may or may not pay to these matters. Divestment is nothing but the redirection of the attention of the ego to itself. Attention does not create the structure to which it attends; in the present case, that structure of ego is inherently not susceptible to creation or generation. Attention only renders explicit what is there implicitly anyway.

Jean-Paul Sartre argues otherwise in *The Transcendence of the Ego*.[1] Since I am never explicitly aware of my own ego when I am engrossed in perception or action, but only when I reflect upon myself, then, he argues, the ego is nothing but a "by-product" of, or is constituted through, that reflection. My ego *is* only when I adopt the peculiar secondary attitude of "reflection," whereupon for the duration of that reflection "I" emerge as a quasi-thing, an "opacity" in the transparency of pure intentionality and consciousness. The "I" that so emerges is at the same time a "public" object about which others can help inform me, a "psychological identity" with its own past, present, future, and hidden character.

Now in all of this there surely is something true, even though it hardly has the consequences Sartre finds. Certainly if I am reading a book, my attention is on what the book is saying and not upon myself reading a book, a form of self-consciousness that would prevent me from reading at all. From such considerations, Sartre concludes that Husserl's insistence that acts of intentionality are acts of a transcendental ego is inconsistent with his general thesis of intentionality, which Sartre sees as indicating that consciousness is exhausted in its intentionality and its projects directed into the world. For Sartre, primordial consciousness—that is, consciousness that has not explicitly adopted the artificial mode of "reflection"—

[1] Jean-Paul Sartre, *The Transcendence of the Ego,* trans. Forrest Williams and Robert Kirkpatrick (New York: Noonday Press, 1957).

is inherently egoless or impersonal. But Husserl never said that consciousness is exhausted in its intentionality, only that it always is also intentional. It need not always intentionally direct itself toward objects; it may also intentionally reflect upon itself. Further, the intentional act must proceed from some spontaneous agent; namely, the ego. And still further, if it animates something with meaning there must be something there to be animated; namely, the "hyletic stratum." All of this complexity is lost in Sartre's analysis, which simply identifies intentionality with consciousness and consigns the remaining features to another ontological domain, that of the *en soi*. To be sure, this simplification serves his own ontological interests in finding but two modes of being, *en-soi* and *pour-soi*. He therefore proposes an impossible task for himself: provided with being-in-itself, about which nothing can be said, and being-for-itself, which is radical nothingness, he must try to characterize the phenomena of the world. But a vocabulary of two terms, plus their various combinations and permutations, would hardly seem rich enough to permit anyone to say anything of detailed precision about anything; and as a result, the value of Sartre's detailed analyses rests not so much on these ontological terms as on his own psychological insight, which has its source elsewhere.

To return to the question of the ego, if being in itself and being for itself or nonbeing look like exhaustive contradictories, it remains to be seen whether consciousness, for all its "nihilating" acts, is simply to be identified with nonbeing, and on that ground it may be evacuated of its own ego, which now finds itself on the other side as a "being," full of "opacity," and a "quasi-public object," in principle "mundane." No doubt at all, there is a dimension of the ego that has some such character: the ego defined as myself with my past, with my dispositions, habits, and tendencies, and as I am for another. But the ego so defined is not the divested transcendental ego, but rather a solidified composition of that ego along with certain formations of it owing to its accidental mundane existence.

And as for Sartre's argument that I am not aware of my ego so long as I am engrossed in action, but only when I reflect, the chief interest in this situation emerges from what I discover when I do reflect. So long as I do not objectify myself but recover myself in a divesting reflection, what I then become aware of is a "myself" that of its very nature cannot be the product of my own attention, but which essentially and eternally is there, hence radically independent of the very act of attention by which I apperceive it. The I that I reflectively discover is identical with the I that was ignored while it was engrossed in objectivity, but only "implicitly" there. At no time do I have the consciousness that my various acts of intentional engrossment belong to nobody; of course they are and were all mine, acts of the very me that now is explicitly apperceived. The implicit awareness that the ego always has of itself, moreover, should not be confused with "unconsciousness." The pair "implicit-explicit" refers to modes of consciousness itself and is not synonymous with "unconscious-conscious."

And so while the ego eternally is, it need not perpetually notice itself. But whenever it does, in divestment from what it is not, it finds itself as that which always is. It can be lost in its projects, intoxicated with love, maddened with pain, or dreaming away its life; and yet all of these activities are but so many acts in existence and in time of an ego that in itself eternally is, and in that capacity is independent of existence and of time.

And so, if my "normal" situation is engrossment in existence, one first but decisive step will be to divest myself of
existence, of what is not me, an act that discloses that which
is capable of having an existence, of being engrossed, of forgetting itself, and of deceiving itself about what it is and
what it is not.

3

The Life of
the Transcendental Ego

The Existence of an Absolute?

IF I DIVEST myself in attention of all that is not me, I am then in reflexive attention only myself. Such an identity is essentially absolute—that is, dependent upon nothing else for its being—and accordingly essentially eternal; that is, not successive to itself and nothing remotely like a process or career in time. The divested ego *is,* but its mode of being is independent of that other mode of being, "existence" or "life," which shall preoccupy us from now on. The self, as we have been considering it, is an eternal singular; ontologically, it can find within it nothing but itself, no God or superior subjectivity, no external nature, no world, and no other selves. Ontologically, therefore, it is final and in no sense derived or dependent upon anything in front of it or behind it. As such, it has considered itself eternally and not existentially. It is neither alive nor dead; it simply is. Needless to say, it has as yet no biography; but it is capable of engrossing itself in existence.

Once it has divested itself of its existence, in the way we have been discussing, the recovery of its existence is not particularly difficult; it requires only a relaxation from the strain of divestment enacted earlier. I already am alive, of course, and the conscious recovery of that life as a theme can only appear as an obvious relief. And yet, dialectically considered, the reinvestment of the ego with the world presents a momentary problem. How indeed can that which is absolute and eternal, in which there is nothing but self, be capable of existence? Is there not a flat contradiction in terms involved here? I believe not, if we are careful to preserve a few distinctions. The self is a singular absolute; it therefore depends on nothing but itself. But to say that it depends on nothing else does not imply that it cannot have nondependent—that is, accidental—relations to what is not itself. Its accidental relations to what is other are accidental precisely to its own absolute nature; that is, not necessary for its own being. They are what "comes" to it (*accidere*), what "happens" to it, where it "finds" itself miraculously, without in any way being deducible from its own nature. Hence, as absolute, the ego does not live, and as alive, it is not absolute; but that can hardly prevent the same singularity from sustaining these two relations, the relation to itself as absolute and to others as relative to them. And, in its relation to those others, it itself becomes relative; that is, it now considers itself in its accidental, existential relations to others. There is then no logical flaw in considering a singular entity in two respects: as related to itself, and as related to what is not itself. Phenomenologically, this means nothing more than a reintroduction into the field of attention of what has just been excluded; in short, absolute reflexivity gives way to the intentional life of consciousness.

That its existence, its life with others, is accidental to its own nature is itself a logical necessity, based simply upon a discrimination of modes of being and modes of consideration. But it coincides as well with what everybody knows; if the *existence* of an eternal ego were not accidental to it but implied by its very nature, then indeed its *life* would be eternal, and each of us would be required upon pain of violating logic to live forever. Happily, this is neither possible nor necessary.

These dialectical considerations can be illustrated by common experience. What, dialectically considered, is the "other" to self is, of course, everything in the world. That everything in the world is other to the self, taken in its absolute intimacy, is in fact the dominant sentiment of philosophers, poets, and children, who again and again reexperience with astonishment the most ordinary things. The world becomes miraculous, strange, and uncanny, no matter how often it has been seen before. Nor can the poetic sense of the miraculous and strange be refuted by recalling to the poet that he has indeed seen that very thing a thousand times before; it is not this comparison he has in mind. The thing is strange—that is, other to —something absolute, and not to its previous appearances. The poet reexperiences the primordial encounter of absolute subjectivity with its absolute other, the world. This radical otherness is itself grounded on the truth that anything objectively encounterable can be encountered only as an opacity measured against the self's own lucidity; the domain of existence must appear strange. Or, in the view of the surrealists, all other things are marvelous and beautiful. No spirit alone with itself would possibly have invented them; they are those othernesses that always and necessarily appear strange to the eternal ego.

No matter how often they are seen, they remain strange. Hence it would be an odd view that saw the fundamental metaphysical strangeness of the world, based as it is on essential conditions, as dependent on nothing but a lapse of memory or a lack of familiarity. Philosophy, said Aristotle, begins in wonder; he did not add that the progress of thought served to extinguish that wonder. No doubt there is a certain puzzlement that can be relieved by "explanations"; but wonder is not exactly puzzlement as to what caused what, but a reexperience of a primordial distance that separates the intimacy of self and the otherness of the domain of existence.

Existence is our name for the domain of being where *something can happen*. Nothing happens in the domain of absolute being; it is eternally what it is. And nothing happens in the domain of ideal essences, where each eternally implies whatever it implies. Life is not there, but where something happens, and that happening must necessarily be an accident to whatever it happens to. If it were not accidental, then it would be derivable from the very nature of the existent to which it was happening; in short, it would be implied by that thing's own nature. But "implication" returns us to the domain of ideal essence. And so whatever happens to the ego must necessarily be a surprise to it, necessarily unforeseeable. The sense of accident, chance, or chaos, all taken as synonymous, has nothing whatsoever to do with the question whether there is some universal objective determinism in nature.

On the one hand, what I experience so long as I am not reflexively grasping myself must necessarily be other to myself, and therefore not deducible from myself; if not deducible, then indeed it must be accidental to myself. Only under such conditions could I experience anything at all. This circumstance, which is phenomenologically certain, is quite different from another matter: whether the thing I experience was or was not necessitated by other things in the objective world, by some supposed law. In any event, it was not necessitated by my subjectivity, and consequently, in relation to that subjectivity, it must appear as an accidental other, even though it may have been necessitated by its own objective causes. Universal determinism may be a fascinating hypothesis to those who feel themselves able to survey the whole universe or to those who know what the universe must be. From my own point of view, whatever the results of that dispute may be, there must still remain the possibility of accidental encounters—that is, encounters not derivable from the natures of those who experience them, and therefore accidental to them. The most primordial stratum of experience, then, is that of the strange and miraculous. It remains irreducible to prediction and knowledge and comprehension; existence logically is the work of chaos.

The life of the transcendental ego, therefore, is its plunge into chaos. Religiously and mythically, it is the "fall." Without that fall, the self would not exist at all; it would perpetually and externally reside within itself. No one knows whether he will exist the next moment, or if he does, what he will see or what he will do; the "one" who does not know this but can experience it with wonder is the singular transcendental ego that each of us is.

Ontologically, existence is that domain in which each thing is what it is because of another thing. No single thing, taken in itself, can exist. The domain therefore is filled with "finite" existents, each of which is what it is by virtue of others. Existence can never be the predicate of a single finite thing; it names rather its membership in a domain of existents, each of which is in the same boat. Existence, then, is a predicate of a finite member of a field of other singular things; only together can they exist. And to each existent thing, its existence comes to it by chance. Insofar as it has sentience, each must experience its existence as the gift of chaos.

Engrossment

An ego once divested of existence now becomes engrossed in it; in a word, it chooses existence. "Chooses" might appear an odd term for the relation of a self to its own existence. But we now are considering that fine point where the absolute falls into existence, or engrosses itself in the domain of the chaotic, and we must do justice to two facts: (1) nothing other to the self can compel or "cause" the ego to exist: and (2) one could make an empirical case for egos that, having had some taste of existence, refuse to have anything further to do with it. Such egos find themselves in mental wards. The fundamental withdrawal or ontological distaste is unmistakable; they can hardly wait to abandon the whole domain and "be by themselves." And to any perceptive eye, there are other forms of the rejection of existence, some enormously "successful." But my present intention is not to moralize on the question, but rather to note that existence is, after all, a matter of choice; or, if "choice" seems to connote some deliberative act based on the conscious weighing of alternatives, then perhaps "consent" or "agreement." In any event, the transcendental ego exists only in its own freedom; it need not exist, and retains at all times the power of withdrawing itself from existence. The ego in its transcendental character need hardly consider itself the unwilling passenger on some unsafe boat, shooting the rapids willy-nilly; it can depart at any time of its own choice.

At this particular moment of our analysis, we find ourselves again as much with dialectical deductions in consciousness as with experiences phenomenologically demonstrable. Again, the great poets have said everything relevant. The moment when the self chooses the universal conditions of existence is articulated in "moods." Moods can be occasioned by just about anything, but they all express the ontological stance of the transcendental ego facing life as such; that is, the necessary ontological conditions of existence. Toward these conditions the ego or "soul" takes a stance, and that stance is experienced as a "mood" or "attitude." To the Schopenhauers, the necessary conditions of existence are intolerable, and so, necessarily, they envisage alternatives: a "life" lived outside of life in the contemplation of ideal form, or an asceticism that finally evaporates the very will to exist. To the Whitmans, on the contrary, everything is beautiful just as it is; there is no need to change anything. What is left but to celebrate every river and stream, every city, every person, just as they all are? The great pessimists and optimists clearly live in universal attitudes toward a totality of existence; and equally clearly, no particular experience could defeat them. What we see here is a transcendental ego taking a position toward existence as a whole, an attitude or mood not in the least dictated by that existence or anything in it, but created freely within the self. Euphoria and melancholy: neither can defend itself by anything within life; both arise from a self that has chosen to exist in a certain way and always in a totality. It is always life as a whole that is felt in such moods. Clearly, then, it is quite possible for an ego to choose or take one among many possible attitudes toward its life as a whole. And, of course, there are in addition equally interesting attitudes that are selective; egos that choose selective attitudes do not have an *a priori* feeling toward life as a whole, but instead discriminate. These are the ones that can choose between "good" and "evil," "beautiful" and "ugly," who are engrossed in particularities. And if the Whitmans and the Schopenhauers seem more "metaphysical," the Shakespeares, who are engrossed in the particularities of life without summary, also have their metaphysical moods, never quite so florid as those of the great simplifiers, but with their own authenticity. In any event, the way in which the absolute ego engrosses itself in the general domain of existence, or the conditions under which it does so, mark that strange point where the ego transcendentally affirms itself by "choosing" to engross itself in the general domain called "existence." This choice always manifests a style or horizon within which further choices are indeed only specifications.

Which "Other"?

If to exist at all is to exist through another, the kind of other becomes decisive for the kind of existence that emerges. If my engrossment engrosses itself simply in an indeterminate "other," a "something else," then the sole aspect of myself that exists for me is my "otherness" to it as such; in a word, my "bare" existence. The dimension of my own existence is a function of the dimension of otherness that exists for me. If my world is a world of things, I am reciprocally conscious of myself as a "thing" that yet is none of those other things. If my horizon of otherness is nature, I locate myself in that nature as another nature. If it is society, I locate myself as a social existent within that society. My engrossment in another singular person in turn enables me to exist as a singular person myself. Each horizon of otherness then discloses mutually what in that world and what in me becomes existent.

Corresponding to various dimensions in the world are various dimensions of engrossment for which there can be that world, and various dimensions in the ego that enacts those engrossments. And since, for its part, the ego that thus engrosses itself in its world is an absolute, neither it nor its modes of intentionality nor the world is exhaustible. The inexhaustibility of existence is a correlate of the absolute character of the ego that exists. Any catalog of dimensions of the ego, types of intentionality, or types of world offers nothing but schemata, provisionally useful for some purposes but utterly deceptive if they are taken as exhaustive of their subject matter. The absolute ego and its possible world cannot in principle be exhausted by any table of finite or determinate categories; they look exhaustive only through the use of empty places in the table, which complete the schematism only through a nonsignificative term. Hence while a whole seems to be exhausted through some such schematism as "subject" and "nonsubject," contradictories that exhaust their own universe of discourse, what could be more apparent than that "nonsubject" has no definite signification, but includes absolutely everything with one exception, "subject"? On the other hand, terms such as "subject" and "object" do not together constitute a logical whole, since it cannot be demonstrated that they constitute contradictories; they are, in effect, nothing but contraries envisaged from the point of view of the subject.

Hence "subject" and "object" are indexical terms, denoting an abstract opposition between an ego and its world, without in the least determinately characterizing the ego, the object, or their mode of opposition. The ego can live in many worlds, or many dimensions of the world; there is a strict correlation between the depth of existence of the ego and the depth of its world. The "stages" in depth of either world, engrossment, or ego are correlative and emerge reciprocally; yet it would be futile to attempt anything like a complete morphology of the matter.

To illustrate this dialectical thesis phenomenologically, let us consider a mind engrossed in the abstract analysis of ideal mathematical relations, which is itself "idealized" in that engrossment; only that dimension of the ego which is itself "performing" the abstraction is activated, or exists. Meanwhile, for the "human world," it is "absentminded." It would be absurd not to recognize the gulf that separates such an engrossment from that of a lover, a statesman, a soldier in battle, or a Thoreau, whose world was split between an ideal transcendentalism more or less Indian and the world of beavers, squirrels, and the natural things in his woods.

And yet it is instructive to notice that even in these exalted, ideal flights out of the human world, there frequently remains the intention to bring back what has been seen to that very human world from which it has flown or upon which it casts its jaundiced eye. Sometimes the direction this intention takes is less than edifying, as when human logicians dispute the priorities of their inhuman discoveries; sometimes it is paradoxical, as when bitter denunciations of human lives are not particularly well received by their intended victims. It would certainly be an oversimplification to find the chief motive for this intention always in some anxiety for human recognition. But this tendency can serve to instruct us in the power of that motive: what is at stake is the human existence of a man among his fellows; and it is that mutual human existence which serves as the platform from which he can direct his eyes elsewhere or upon occasion back to where he himself is. The logic of the logician must remain untouched by that anxiety; and yet the intention behind his effort manifests at one and the same time the pursuit of an ideal clarity untouched by human existence and the celebration of that very accomplishment in the human world. Without the engrossment in the ideal, nothing would be seen; the logic would degenerate into an uncontrolled polemic. But with engrossment alone we should never see what the logician had seen; he as logician would have effectively vanished from the world.

But all such worlds, intentionalities, and correlative dimensions of the ego are but abstractions when compared with that ultimately concrete horizon of existence within which I, an absolute singular, exist absolutely singularly with another subjectivity, who in turn mutually exists as an absolute singularity, absolutely singularly, with me. If "ego" seems an appropriate term for a person taken in absolute reflexivity, it loses that appropriateness here. Now it is a "person," personally existing with another person; and here, to "exist with" means that the person of each has become essential to the existence of the other. Hence when two persons become essential to each other's lives, or rather when they merge in a mutual and reciprocal personal existence, then in that reciprocal intersubjective life an ontological finality exists, which constitutes the world of both. Measured against this, all other modes of existence represent so many forms of abstraction, no matter how passionately they may be pursued. The universal name for this final, personal engrossment in which each subjectivity finds the other essential is, of course, love. The lovers are inseparable not in fact but as factors in the mutual life; in fact, of course, they are subject to the same overarching chaos that defines the entire domain of existence, which never fails to contribute its own note of poignancy to what also is absolute.

Love, then, is that form of mutual existence of transcendental egos in which each finds the other essential to that mutuality, which expresses both the transcendental character of those in love and the existential chaos in which that finality emerges. Final personality emerges in its clearest form, and the whole affair can be understood only ontologically, as a mode of mutual being. Nothing could be more absurd than efforts to analyze love as if it were an "emotion" rather than a form of existence—an emotion, moreover, that had its locus in one or the other of the lovers. Emotions may certainly be felt for love, as everyone knows, but to regard love as an emotion or feeling in one or the other is to look not at love but at deceived or imagined love, in which there may be no corresponding reality. And so Spinoza: "Love is a feeling of pleasure accompanied by the idea of another as its cause"! We shall look into the matter in detail below.

An A Priori *Sociology*

The sole domain of existence that is adequate to the persons of those in that domain is that of reciprocal recognition. I am not a person among things, among animals, among abstractions; none of these worlds elicits anything from me except my corresponding dimension as a thing, an animal, or an abstraction. I am most personally existent when I exist in reciprocal acknowledgment with other persons. I then live with "others," but now with "others" who are themselves conscious of my consciousness; hence subjectivity can exist only with and for other subjectivities. My subjectivity is nothing to the world of nature, although it may be something to me. My personal subjectivity exists for me only when it is acknowledged by other personal subjectivities who are acknowledged by me. As a result, the only field of existence in which I can be a personal subjectivity is the world of other persons. If this domain is called the "social," it is clear that human existence is only for human existents; the entire domain of human social existence means nothing whatsoever to things outside it. As Santayana says, the whole history of human life will at some time be for nature nothing but a peculiar shadow left by our ruined cities on the face of the moon. And yet although this obvious truth is apt to overimpress some naturalists who take the side of the moon, it can hardly have the implication that human history is really nothing but the way it appears to the moon. It is not that for us so long as we remain persons; and what it is for us is its final sense for us. The very essence of human life, what we are for one another, arises and ends there; what our lives are is what we are for one another and not what traces we leave upon the moon, which, after all, has never been granted citizenship in any community except under the guise of some personification.

Why human existence should think so little of itself as to be depressed by its transiency, by the lack of recognition with which nature greets us, by the infinitesimal dimensions of its sidereal scene, would itself make an interesting subject for transcendental psychoanalysis, which would excavate the secret intentionalities, the disappointments, and the inherent anxiety involved in life. And yet if autobiography is taken with sufficient seriousness—taken, that is to say, ontologically—it is hardly the human scene that is dwarfed by infinite time and infinite space; it is rather all those natural infinities that can now be put in their proper place as the background of something infinitely richer, deeper, and more fragile, our own lives.

The life of the transcendental ego, then, is played out with and for others; it is essentially "social." Considered against the backdrop of stars or subatomic events, it is nothing; and indeed it is nothing to them. But why should we adopt their point of view in the quarrel? We can remain ourselves in any event, and if the whole human drama, autobiographically considered, is as nothing to the world of nature, then indeed, reciprocally, all of nature is nothing but the domain in which we play out our own personal destinies. That these dramas are those of absolute selves saves something of their significance for eternity. Nothing in nature has that significance; or when nature does gather itself together to become a self, what has emerged except ourselves, who now reflect on the whole matter?

PART II

What Is Man?

4

What Is Man?

Knowing and Know-How

IT WOULD, of course, be absurd to "protest against science" and its most appropriate product for us, the machine. The natural sciences are but extensions of our legitimate interest in the workable side of nature; and if someone should prefer to remain ignorant of that side of nature, we must grant him his heart's desire and leave him to the consequences. For any single person to choose ignorance would doubtless be inconsequential; for a society as a whole to remain ignorant of the natural sciences could hardly be counted a blessing, and no such society at the present time could survive except on tolerance of those societies that did encourage such an interest.

The product of the natural sciences that is most appropriate for us is not knowledge about nature itself, I believe, but rather *know-how;* that is, certain rules for manipulating certain types of natural things under certain conditions. Knowing that certain substances will explode under certain conditions is practical know-how of a useful sort, but it hardly brings us closer to comprehending what any natural being is unless we simply decide to call such an acquaintance with natural things "comprehension." In any event, it is not comprehension or understanding in the sense that it enables us legitimately to say that we comprehend or understand ourselves or one another. I shall return to this later; but for the moment, let us confine our concern to the technical management of natural things for the production of results we desire, which finds its fulfillment in machines of various sorts. No sooner have we multiplied machines, and thereby transformed our environment until we are virtually living in an artificial world, than some arise to protest against the machine. A good deal of this protest seems somewhat archaic and little more than a matter of preference, perfectly legitimate as such but not exactly obligatory for people of other tastes. If some prefer to write their poetry with quills rather than typewriters, or gallop across town on horseback to fetch their potatoes rather than phone for a delivery by truck, their time is their own and each may employ it as he will. But if he acts on principle, then he must be consistent; we shall deny him aspirin for his headaches, ether for his surgery, electricity for illumination. It is difficult to know exactly how far his asceticism will reach. I for one shall not follow him, for under present historical conditions his trail leads not at all into an idyllic rapport with a natural environment, but straight into the most artificial environment of all, the mental ward.

If the protest against "science" and the "machine" so stated looks somewhat childish, perhaps we can relocate its intended thrust. It could hardly be authentic knowledge of nature that anyone would wish to reject, but rather an unauthentic by-product, the illegitimate extension of the methods of natural science to subject matter of every sort, and the ensuing philosophical notion that our understanding of all things must be modeled on our knowledge of those things in nature that have yielded to the procedures of natural science. This is not natural science, but rather a philosophy or perhaps a religion modeled upon natural science, and, to anticipate our conclusions, a highly defective one at that. The philosophical examination of the natural sciences is one thing; it helps to define what its methods are: observation, experiment, and prediction in the spirit of objectivity and impersonality. But to adopt a conviction that such procedures and the particular form of know-how that can be expected to emerge from them are universally applicable to all domains of being—that scientific knowledge is knowledge *par excellence,* that nothing is known unless it is known by these procedures, that nothing is unless it falls in the same domain as those things that are usefully observed by the experimental sciences—this far outruns science itself, to become not the philosophy of the natural sciences, but rather natural science as a philosophy.

It is from this quarter that one hears such remarks as that "science has outstripped the humanities," that "ethics must catch up with the natural sciences," that we may hope for insight into the human condition when we too are subjected to an examination conducted according to the experimental method, that mind has now been shown to be nothing but a somewhat complicated computer, that science shows God does or does not exist, and so on and on. This particular form of madness reaches its practical zenith with the wish to entrust political decisions to experts in political science, sociology, and group psychology, as though the free and responsible decision as to what we shall communally make of ourselves were a matter of experimental conclusions or scientific expertise. It goes without saying that substantial knowledge from any quarter is always welcome; but it should also go without saying that no knowledge of anything we have ever done or are now doing presents us with anything but a moral problem and not a solution: which of it shall we reaffirm, which change? And that particular decision can never be the logical conclusion of any scientific syllogism. To be better informed of our individual and social condition and of the probable consequences of our actions is one thing; to suppose that information of itself determines our response is quite another. This is, of course, an old saw in philosophy, but it is frequently forgotten in the enthusiasms of those who talk of "human engineering," "programmed lives," "controlled environments," and the rest. The saddest spectacle, however, is offered not by those who happen to think these things possible, but by those who dearly wish them to be true. What are we to say of any mind whose most ardent wish is not to be itself? Unamuno once heard a popular lecturer proving to his listeners that they were absolutely mortal. What puzzled Unamuno was not that they all appeared to accept this—for after all, the whole question is of enormous difficulty—but that they threw their hats into the air, cheering their own future death.

In any event, let us focus the discussion on one central issue: What is man? I haven't the slightest intention of "answering" this question, but I would like to advance some reasons for regarding it as unanswerable in the way it is put, and to suggest that the question itself arises from a false premise. There can be no true answer to the question "What is man?" But there is another way in which that question can be put that transforms it into something more profitable: What are *men*? What have men done? And eventually: Who am I? The shift of emphasis is from something called "man" to singular individuals; from doctrines of a common essence or nature shared by all to singular lives lived; and finally from a perpetual obsession with what *other* men must be like to a choice of what I as an existing man must *do*. I wish I could claim this as a personal discovery; but unfortunately for that ambition, the Delphic oracle three thousand years ago initiated philosophy with the commandment "Know thyself." It did not say, "Know nature," or "Know everybody else," or "Know yourself as though you were one object among many"; it certainly did not command us to be psychologists of ourselves. In fact, like all oracles, it presented us with an enigma and left us to do the best we could with it. What it did not command is far clearer than what it might have wished as a fulfillment. But the initiator of Western philosophy, Socrates, took it with absolute seriousness; it is not at all certain that he was not the last who did. What does seem certain is that the natural sciences as well as certain modes of philosophical thought are virtually designed to make us forget who we are. There not only are, but always have been, other modes of thought that do not falsify us or betray our condition. These other modes of thought, which I shall try to specify in a moment, are frequently considered, especially today, as "informal" or "bad science" by philosophizing scientists, or as "merely human opinion" by devoted theologians, or as something "merely autobiographical" by philosophers hypnotized by universal doctrine. But there are some reasons for believing that the autobiographical, the biographical, and the poetic or humanistic modes of insight and expression are very far from being informal or uncontrolled science, and that they are not "merely" anything else at all, but rather the most faithful, subtle, and profound comprehension we have of the only thing in the world of being of which we can have any comprehension at all: ourselves.

The Natural Sciences and the History of Man

The natural sciences, of course, aim at the laws of nature, and perpetually seek more and more general laws under which more particular laws can be subsumed. These laws or hypotheses are tested in observations, experiments, and predictions, according to well-worked-out methods. We can know how and why various classes of natural things change only after we have watched them under a variety of artificially varied conditions. We formulate our guess as to the aspects of their total environment responsible for the changes we observe, reproduce the conditions we have selected, and see if the predicted results occur. When they do, we are happy, and we formulate the results as a law, theory, or hypothesis that has a degree of probability to it. Things that are susceptible to this approach we call "natural"; and it is immediately apparent that a scientific law can apply only to those things or events that follow a general law or rule. To follow a general law is the same as to be repeatable; if the conditions are repeated, then the identical effects will follow. In short, if, in the whole sphere of being, some things are repeatable or cyclic, then we can hope to discover the law of their repetition. Natural things clearly are cyclic, and equally clearly their law is susceptible of being found out. But simply because certain natural things and events in being are cyclic, we have as yet no ground for assuming that everything that is cyclic or repetitive follows a general law, and therefore that the law of its cycle can be found out. That is an enormous and illegitimate extension from the domain of nature to everything in being itself; in short, this philosophy of naturalism, which is not itself a natural science but either a philosophy or religion of nature, surely rests on nothing more than the wish to see a correspondence between everything that is and certain cyclic events in nature.

On the other hand, there is a very conspicuous domain of existence that in its first appearance, at least—and I believe in its last truth also—is not cyclic and repetitive: the domain of human history. In this domain, in contrast to the domain of nature, we encounter precisely the opposite: the perpetual emergence of novelty, the unpredicted, the explosive, a scene of choice and decision, a scene in which one kind of being, man, has to decide what he will do, what kind of life he will live, and what he will make of himself. And when we find societies that do not offer us this image, we are instantly inclined to think of them as primitive, not yet historical, asleep, and analogous to a beehive or anthill, caught up not in history, but in natural cycles of birth, life, decay. There have indeed been societies that have had this aspect, ancient Egypt and ancient China, societies that do not seem to us explosive or dynamic, but which aimed at an eternal mythical recurrence. Whether they were so in fact to those who lived in them is another matter; it might very well be that the inertia and cyclic repetitiveness we see in them are due to the vast historical distance that separates us from them. But perhaps that was exactly how they were. In any event, our conclusion is the same: the historical is inherently the life that men make for themselves by their free decisions, and therefore is inherently developmental and not cyclic, although development here does not necessarily mean "progressing" or "improving," but has only the minimal sense of a certain restlessness. If natural things have their lives already laid out in the gene structure of their natural heredity, man finds that he is, in Sartre's phrase, condemned to be free, so that even when he chooses to live according to some mythical cycle, he is only making one more free choice, which must constantly be reconfirmed and enforced by free decisions.

And so when we recall where we are in life, is it not clear that our actions are not effects of conditions, but rather free responses to them? And if frequently we decide to respond to a situation in the same way we responded earlier to a situation of the same sort, and hence decide to become repetitive and cyclic, in fact we have freely chosen to follow a rule, and could just as freely have chosen not to follow it; hence the rule has the force of only describing one more free choice, not determining that choice. History therefore appears to us as a domain of human action, which means free response and choice among alternatives open in the unique situation within which the choice is made. Far from being cyclic and repetitive, it is rather the field of human creation. The sober truth is that when human life is cyclic and repetitive, it is boring; and while much of it may indeed be boring, it is not then at its best, and there is nothing to be drawn from the natural sciences that compels it to be so.

There is a second reason why the methods of the natural sciences are the least appropriate approaches to the inner sense of human life. Science as such, and therefore natural science too, aims at something universally true. Its proper subject matter is *classes* of things, not things in their singularity. This is in turn a function of its interest in laws or rules. On the other hand, human existence is inherently an interest, choice, and preoccupation with the singular. Human beings first and foremost give themselves proper names. Our cities have proper names, and all the parts of nature closest to our concerns have proper names. The domain of human existence is a domain of singularities, the sun and the moon, the earth, ourselves in our singularities. Our interest in existence is in what we must choose, alternatives that are themselves singular possibilities, not generalities. Our history is the record of what singular nations and singular men have singularly done. And for each, there is always his own singular death, which no one may die for him. In short, the essence of human existence is in its unrepeatability, its singularity, and its historical record; it is not in the universal, the general, the type, or anything designatable by common nouns. It is perfectly true that any singular is an example of a common type; but it is also something very distinct from that type, and meanwhile the existential, active interest of human existence is not and cannot be an interest in the universal, but only in the singular. And so while my own death is most certainly an instance of the universal notion "death," it is not with respect to that universal that I direct my efforts to live, but toward my own singular existence with others. Death as such, the death that is common to us all, is not the issue for anyone's existence; it is only the singular event, my death and your death, that can logically function as a possibility for choice or avoidance. Similarly, if I go to a party, I go to be with other singular people, each with his proper name; if all I were interested in were the universal, "man," I need never stir out of my room. I myself exemplify that universal, and what reason would I legitimately have to look at others?

Hence the very posing of the question "What is man?" is itself an invitation to forget who we are; we are not merely examples of that universal category, but chiefly singular individuals existing mortally with other singular individuals, all of us having to choose freely whom we are to become and what we are to do. There is no point at all in trying to find something called the "definition of man" when the whole interest, concern, and zest of human existence is precisely in a particular existence, our own, which has to decide which possible essence or definition it will wear. To attempt therefore to grasp the very essence of man is to attempt to grasp what is most irrelevant to the human scene, and what it would be fatal to take seriously. Am I not invited by any such pretended definition to think I already possess the significance of every lived human existence, all those that have been, running back to the ape man, as well as those now alive and those to come? All we can conclude is that any definition sufficiently universal to encompass the significance of every lived existence as well as the open future of man would have to be so general as to be pertinent to no single existence.

And so I conclude that there can be no pertinent law of human existence, no definition of man, and that if there is any rule at all in the domain of human existence, it is the simple law of free creation; that is, the law that here there is no law.

Morality

If there is no definable human nature, neither can there be anything like "the" human situation, "the" human predicament, or "the" human problem, but only singular situations, predicaments, and problems, which may accidentally and without any necessity be shared by none, few, or many. A situation, predicament, or problem must be the situation, predicament, or problem of someone, and if the decisive thing in men is their freedom and singularity, they are by that token free to create their own problems, take or leave what they like in their environment, and involve themselves in whatever they like as a predicament.

It also follows from the freedom and singularity of human existences that there can be no universally valid values or moral laws, no universal sense of life that is "true," and no universally binding religious commandments. As for values, they must be valuable for someone or they aren't values at all, but merely possible states of affairs. Now a possible state of affairs may be a possible option, but it becomes a value only when opted for. The only sort of being that can make such free options is a singular man or a singular community of men; option is an act of existence. But universal values or moral laws can have as their logical correlate only universal man or the universal community, the essence of man and his society. But no such essence could be born, live, or die, and it certainly could have no history. Nor could it actually opt for anything. If by chance there are certain features we all factually share, that itself is of no importance, since no reason can be given why the features we do share must be of more importance to us than those we do not. The real import and eventual tyranny of moralism emerges here: it is the premise of the moral argument that it is itself immoral not to institute in ourselves that universal essence preconceived by the moralist. Insofar as that essence of man or society is a genuine essence, it must logically exclude the very historical becoming of men that is their lives. Or if the very generality of the essence does not exclude it, it ignores it. In either case, is it not plain that while it is perfectly possible to opt to become some such type, there can be no universally binding law compelling existing men to do so? And with that, the pretended universality of morality vanishes.

It should be understood that these remarks are intended to deprive any morality of universal validity by showing that any value it offers becomes a value solely through historical, subjective, and existential choices. Values have no authority other than that conferred upon them by these choices. Neither pure reason nor natural science can validate any possible state of affairs as moral or valuable. The argument thus is intended to state certain final things about the existential source of value. Chapter 9 will discuss the subject in further detail.

The argument is not intended as an invitation to social anarchy or personal disintegration. These, like their contraries, social law and personal coherence, represent possible options that can be neither attacked nor defended by a consideration of the free origins of all values. Similarly, if no reason can be given why I should either live or die other than my own free option, that circumstance hardly requires me to choose suicide in order to prove my freedom, like the heroes of Dostoevsky. Men are surely free to order or disorder their communities as seems best to them; but this hardly supplies a justification for preferring no order at all. In short, the intent of the argument is to uncover the source of value, personal or social. That source is not to be found in either science or the pure reason of philosophy. The argument therefore releases us to the responsibilities of our own choices.

The same conclusion must be drawn for religion. If the ultimate significance of human life were the significance it had for God, then it would be God that enjoyed that significance, not living men themselves; and far from conferring a higher dignity on human life, this would remove human dignity altogether, for men would be mere instruments. If a man finds satisfaction in conceiving himself to be an instrument of what he conceives to be divine, and freely chooses to live his life in such a way that it conforms to his sense of a divine commandment, then indeed that is his free choice. But he and he alone is the reflected benefactor, and such a choice has no obligatory force upon others. Others remain free to find no value whatsoever in religious life; they remain human too.

The Humanities

If there is no natural science of human life, and if no light is to be cast upon "the" human condition by notions of what men ought to do, ought to be, ought to wish for, ought to prize, and if no universal sense to all life is to be derived from revelations from God, is not the whole of human existence cast into a rather profound darkness? What light is left to human existences in all their freedom and singularity? But surely men have never lacked awareness of themselves and of one another, and of what they have been about; it is only that that awareness is not expressed in science, moral law, or religion. Is it not rather formulated in that most ancient form of human expression, what we now call the "humanities"? Men have always told each other what they have done, seen, suffered; and one of their chief preoccupations, when they have exhausted themselves in biography, autobiography, and history, is inventing imaginary tales, embroidering on what has been as they dream of what could have been. It is literature, not science, morality, or religion, that speaks most appropriately of human lives in the language closest to those lives. And when literature is purest, when it is not trying to do what it cannot do in any case, it never gives a scientific explanation of anything, it delivers no laws of human existence, it neither urges nor threatens us with anything, and it is least of all an informal sociology talking about the human condition, the human predicament, or human nature as such. Not, of course, that authors haven't done all these things. But when they do, they are not presenting literature in its purest or most authentic form. At its best, literature simply presents or records singular human existences in their singular situations, making their absolute choices of life.

In short, it shows us to ourselves, not in order to teach something about all men, or to moralize, but simply to show what has happened or what might have happened. The showing, or pure expression, raises human existence to explicit consciousness; and that itself, I am convinced, is the only form of comprehension we can achieve or have any good reason to seek. If Shakespeare shows us not the human predicament, and not mankind, but rather Hamlet, a most singular and unrepeatable man, in a most singular and unrepeatable situation, making precisely the existential choices that define Hamlet as Hamlet, then, to the extent that the play is successful, we succeed in comprehending Hamlet. We do not "explain" him, we do not morally judge him; we comprehend him. This comprehension that we can attain in great works of literature, this understanding of the singular existences displayed in them, is knowledge, the best knowledge we can have of ourselves; it has virtually nothing in common with that other form of knowledge of which I spoke earlier, scientific know-how.

I think it would be a vast mistake to consider works of literature as allegories for our time, even when their authors dearly wish them to be so. They may be written in our time or in another; they may present relatively common situations. But their excellence in disclosing the free choices, the actions and sufferings of their heroes has nothing to do with whether the hero or his situation is common or rare. Nor has it anything to do with defining human nature. How indeed can all of us be both K. of *The Trial* and Meursault, *The Stranger?* K. is so ridden with metaphysical guilt that he finally agrees with his executioners, although he has done no wrong; Meursault, on the other hand, has so little feeling of guilt that all the forces of persuasion fail to make him confess any guilt at all, and he goes alone and undaunted to his death, although he has killed a man. Both men, of course, present us with human possibilities; but neither defines the condition of man or human nature, and their value does not lie in some hoped-for contemporary social comment, even if Orson Welles does add a mushroom cloud at the end of his version of *The Trial.*

Would it not be more appropriate, then, to read literature of authentic excellence as disclosing the character, decision, and singular situation of the person who is shown in the particular work, and of him alone, and to rid ourselves once and for all of the ambition to transform these singular illuminations of singular existences into tracts for the times, into contributions to some hoped-for general theory of human nature, into teachings, allegories, and all the rest, which only make us forget who and where we are?

5

Transcendental Love

ROMANTIC LOVE is now regarded by historians of ideas as more or less a creation of the Provençal poets of the thirteenth century; but however this may be, we shall be interested here not so much in its date of origin, or where it may be found, or among whom, or why, as in its phenomenological structure: what is the inner sense of this unique fusion of the transcendental and the erotic? So let us begin by stipulating that the subject matter of our analysis is that species of love which is not exclusively an affair of the sentiments, a bodiless but spiritual affection, or what used to be called Platonic love; nor is it exclusively sexual appetite, the libido, which Freudians devoutly believe is the basic reality at the bottom of all human experience. Nor is it the mechanical addition of animal sex plus spiritual affection, a middle ground that might be thought to be more appropriate but which is simply a confusion of mind. What, then, is romantic love? This will supply our first theme.

If the term "love" is ambiguous, "metaphysics" or the "transcendental" is even worse. One or the other has been used as the name for everything that pretends to be profound as well as everything that philosophies of experience regard as absolute confusion. It has been regarded as rational theology, as armchair physics, as general science, as synthetic *a priori* propositions, as emotional expression pretending to be objective knowledge: in other words, metaphysics has usually been regarded as an abstruse and tedious chain of reasonings leading the mind from what it can sensibly know into an area so remote from our experience and faculties that any extravagant fancy can pass for the truth. Today it is axiomatic among empiricists that metaphysics, whatever else it may suppose itself to be, tries at the very least to talk about what no one can experience, about something that cannot serve to predict future events, cannot be confirmed in any experience, and therefore is a game of words that can be ignored by those interested in the serious purposes of science. But to begin with, I want to stipulate that here "metaphysics" is not the name of any inquiry into language or the methods of the sciences, or any inquiry into metaempirical and hypothetical entities, least of all the content of synthetic *a priori* propositions. I take "metaphysics" to name the effort to disengage from experience something *absolute*. And what is the absolute? Whatever else it is, I shall take the absolute to be that which is final for knowledge, final in value, and final in being—an appearance of the transcendental.

Knowledge is final when our cognition of an object is both adequate to the object itself and known to be adequate. Its truth therefore is not a matter of chance, hypothesis, or external comparisons. Cognition is adequate, absolute, and final when we grasp the object wholly, and know that we grasp it wholly. But can anything be so grasped or known? Isn't there always more to be known about any existent thing, and isn't what we do know merely probably true, true of its object merely hypothetically? The answers to these questions should not be given too rapidly.

Finality in value is, at least formally, easier to define. An absolute or final value is that value which is not a means to another, or a part, phase, or aspect of another, and which is not increased by the addition of any other. Again, *is* there any such value? Or are all claims to final value delusive?

The absolute in being, or ontological finality, is what is self-sufficient. It is what needs nothing else in order to be. It is therefore not a property, accident, phase, moment, abstraction, or part of anything else. Traditionally, this absolute is sometimes called the "real" and is opposed to the merely existent. Candidates for reality are the Good of Plato, the Thought Thinking Thought of Aristotle, the One of Plotinus, Nature or Substance in Spinoza, and, of course, the Absolute Mind in Hegel. But again, to define the real is not immediately to prove that it exists or that it is relevant to or confirmable by anything experienceable.

Such a definition of the final and absolute might seem to confirm the contentions of empirical philosophy. Surely, it seems, there is nothing absolute in experience, and therefore any philosophy of experience can get along quite nicely without it. Hence our preliminary definition of "metaphysics" as the effort to disengage something absolute from experience might seem to name, right at the start, a project that is futile in principle. There is, it is widely believed, a radical incompatibility between the absolute and experience; or, in the theological language of another period, between God and the world.

But is the absolute incompatible with experience? It is certainly incapable of exemplification in *some* experience; but if we are to say it is incompatible with experience as such, we must in all honesty try to look further afield than the experiences that seem to dominate the attention of many empiricists—sensations of white patches, inner feelings of pleasure and pain, and the so-called constructions of these unpromising data into facsimiles of the world. We must look in a different way, too. Our method must be phenomenological: it will attempt to reflect upon experience as experience is given, without presuppositions as to what it *must* contain, what *must* cause it, what relation it can or cannot have to entities independent of it. We shall, in other words, attempt to look at the given as it is given, ascertain its given structure, and then later reflect upon the problems posed by the appearance of such a structure. This procedure seems justified by the obvious truth that one can hardly think about the causes, effects, or possible significance of something until that something has itself been satisfactorily grasped and described.

But what experience shall we choose? This brown desk before me? The inevitable white patch of the blank paper on which I am trying to write? Fortunately there are other matters to reflect upon, and love is one of them. Let us, then, for a moment suspend our convictions about patches of color, sounds, and inner sensations of pleasure and pain, and in the freedom of ignorance look once again at love. When we look at it, we shall at the same time be looking *for* something: its possibility of offering up to reflective attention those metaphysical meanings that confound the finite philosophers of experience. There is no need, for our purposes, in trying to perform the overly ambitious task of developing a total description of love. But we can examine love, not in all of its aspects, but only to see if it may disclose concretely an otherwise formal and ideal meaning, the absolute.

Love might seem to be the least promising experience to examine, since lovers, while in love, are obviously in no mood to reflect upon their love in order to prove a metaphysical thesis. Nevertheless, they have the power of recollection, and besides, they can draw on the reflections of others. There is hardly any other theme in literature about which so much has been written. And so, while it is always the phenomenon itself that alone can justify any description, and to which we must always return, still a vast body of poetic literature furnishes a welcome aid and kind of confirmation. The literature I have in mind is, of course, the ancient myths, lyric love poetry, and classical love letters, and also popular songs and the love letters and mash notes of humble lovers. All of this constitutes a vast body of expression that, while it can be overemphasized, does have its weight. But while we are examining these verbal expressions of love, we may as well say what everyone knows: that their fundamental meaning is neither subtle nor hypothetical. At bottom they all say what every lover finds himself reduced to saying both first and last, "I love you"—nothing more and nothing less. And while we are assembling the evidence, we should include facial expressions, ranging from oblique glances to winks, knowing looks, bedroom eyes, and the infinite variety of smiles, with their overt meanings and with those secret meanings that are nevertheless meant to be understood, as well as gestures and the holding of hands, all of which in their various modulations finally resolve themselves into the kiss and the embrace. Clearly such expressions can assert nothing about love; rather they are all expressions, declarations, or exposures of it. They are at once expressions and acts of love; they articulate or disclose what they accomplish. Hence the well-known preference of lovers for poetry, which, unlike prose, does not assert anything about anything, but rather expresses and articulates its own content.

If first, then, we look at all this utterance, and take care to include only that which expresses the lovers insofar as they are in love, and not insofar as they bicker, are jealous, or also hate one another, we find some remarkable things said. Lovers call each other "divine." It is as if they appeared as gods and goddesses to one another. They say their love was created in heaven; that they have always known one another; that their love is eternal; that only now are they whole, and that they have discovered at last the meaning of life. They are fulfilled, so much so that some lovers form suicide pacts; everything else life could offer would be nothing but an enfeeblement and dissipation. Some such thing is the expression of erotic-romantic love, and in a variety of forms it can be found in Shakespeare, Donne, Goethe, the Brownings, Hart Crane, and the rest, as well as in men who are otherwise not literary. But what a mass of nonsense! our sober common sense exclaims. The poetic expression of romantic love is evidence of nothing more than a temporary loss of reason or a calculated attempt at seduction. No man of common sense would take it seriously. Everyone knows the origin and purposes of such poetry. If a lover has not become unbalanced by desire, or even if he has, what else would he do but deliberately flatter the beloved to the point of intoxication? The sober truth is that from the points of view of both common sense and science, what the lovers say is simply false.

The simplest worldly wisdom knows, for example, that the lovers are not gods, not divine. If our common sense is grounded in religious attitudes, the idea seems positively blasphemous; if not, ludicrous. Animals on two legs who were born and who will die—these are gods? And how could they always have known one another when obviously they hadn't even met the day before yesterday? And how can their love be eternal when, as everyone knows, before one of them has finished declaring love eternal his eye will begin to rove, both lovers will get restless, and tomorrow they will view each other with either hate or indifference? How can this be the meaning of life, when there are so many other pleasures, pleasures certainly less disturbing, less expensive to the spirit, and less turbulent? Finally, can anyone believe that lovers really know one another, when nothing could be clearer to an onlooker than the deceptions they mutually practice? The fond beloved does not know that her lover is also a murderer, or, worse, has another woman on the string. If love is an absolute fulfillment, what about the day that is yet to come?

Biological science reinforces the criticism. It knows perfectly well that love is not eternal, but follows the seasons; it is not made in heaven, but in certain glands; it is a consequence of certain chemical principles, and statistically is the most predictable thing in the world. What is romantic love but the same phenomenon that can be observed among the birds, bees, and worms, now overlaid with poetic rhetoric, owing principally to the human propensity to interpret perfectly natural phenomena in an outrageously metaphysical or religious sense?

Here, then, we have the poets and lovers themselves raving throughout the ages in a language that is frankly metaphysical; we have the man of common sense, who finds the whole thing amusing and perhaps forgivable nonsense; and we have the scientist, who offers a natural description and explanation of the whole business. My own contention is that all of them see something true, and that their views conflict only when one or another of them insists that his own particular perspective is the only valid one. We would know less about the subject if we neglected to view it from any one of these perspectives. We must, then, take the poetic expression of love as a serious addition to our knowledge; we must say that it is not nonsense or false, and that it is not reducible to the other two. In addition to crediting literally what the lovers say and what anyone can confirm for himself, I should like also to maintain that the love that is articulated in romantic poetry has precisely the features we are looking for in our attempt to disengage the absolute within experience, and that, since it offers an entrée into the absolute, it has a necessary priority to either common sense or science, both of which are hopelessly sunk in the finite. It is not they that are capable of discrediting love, but rather love that can discredit their inflated claims.

With this in mind, let us extract a few banalities from everyone's experience and from literature, and after a schematic characterization let us then reflect upon their significance. To begin with, we shall be talking about the passion of love, not about an interest in it, a flirtation with it, not about the sophistication concerning it on which the nineteenth-century French gallant prided himself and with which he invariably escaped. Hegel characterized passion as a total devotion of one's whole heart. In this sense men have a passion for politics, for science, for saintliness, and for other things; but there is no passion for collecting postage stamps or memorizing railroad timetables. Romantic love is love as a passion, not as a passing amusement or as a cathartic for accumulated tensions or as a means of preserving the species, although it may of course also be all of these.

Now any passion can be discussed medically, or it can be observed with amusement from a distance. Insofar as passion is passion, insofar as it is itself, it is obviously not concerned with its own physiological conditions, nor is it an objective "state." A passion is a mode of subjective existence, or life, and its interior structure and meaning are primarily accessible only to the subject existing in that mode. Common-sense observation and medical diagnosis may observe its signs and behavior or its physiological conditions. But signs and physical conditions are, by their very nature, properties of objects; passion is a mode of subjectively lived existence. To this passion, as it is subjectively lived, common sense and science can only allude.

For any primary analysis of passion, therefore, we must locate ourselves within the horizon of the subject existing passionately: we must recover the memories and echoes of passion within ourselves, and see what they disclose. The adoption of the standpoint of the existing subject requires a resolute effort to forget what we suppose we already know and to relive the actual phenomenon as it exists for such a subject, and not as it presents itself to an external observer with common sense or with a degree in biology or psychology.

And what is disclosed to the passion of the lover? Only one thing: the beloved other. Nothing more ought to be said. But we may pause to look at what frequently has been said. The other, it has been claimed, is really given to passion in the form of colored patches and other sense data, combined with inner feelings of pleasure; this is all that is or can be given to sensation, and the rest is pure construction. Now, whatever such reasoning may or may not contribute to the epistemology of hypothetical physical objects, it most certainly does not describe anything remotely like what passion discloses; rather it rests on suppositions as to basic data along with more suppositions as to the processes by which such data are "constructed" into what we are finally to take to be the love of a person. But since the living person must first be given to passion before the supposed accuracy of the reconstruction can be checked, let us quickly put this theory aside until we are in a better position to see where it fails.

Another theory supposes that we apprehend only the physical body, and that the mind of another can only be inferred. But the physical body is a most ambiguous notion. When we refer to it, we suppose ourselves to be on safe ground: are not all physical bodies more or less alike, and is not a theory that is adequate to physical bodies as such adequate to the theory of love, and is not the theory of physical bodies simply a part of physics? Obviously, however, a physical body that is loved is very different from a physical body that is not loved; so different, in fact, that it is hardly appropriate to call it a physical body at all. As we all know, what the lover loves is not just a physical body, but the body of a *person,* and the body of a person is that person's *living flesh.* Living human bodies are not physical bodies at all; a purely physical body is inanimate, lacks a soul. In contrast to a living human body, it is dead. It is characterized by an inherent lack of responsiveness. It is complete within its own cycle of physical influences and is incapable of returning love. Now, it is quite possible to love a physical body that does not express a mind or soul; Krafft-Ebing studied such loves under the label "necrophilia." But our present study is not directed to morbid modifications, interesting as they are. Erotic love is not love of the purely physical; the living human body is its object, and that body is apprehended by passion as the body of a person, as the body enlivened by and expressing another human spirit. To try theoretically to abstract the spirit that lives in the body from the body itself would leave a dead body, and a dead spirit as well.

If the idea of a purely chemical or physical love is absurd, it is equally absurd to fly to the opposite error and, like the medieval ascetics, regard one's own body and that of the other as hindrances to what might otherwise be a purely spiritual affection. For the other mind that is loved is an existing other mind, and how else is it to exist but in and through its body? It is precisely the indwelling of the mind or spirit of the other in his body that transforms that body from an inanimate mass having purely physical properties into a unique living organ of expression. There is also a transcendental dimension to the mind, but all by itself it is not accessible through passion and is not the object of erotic-romantic love. Hence to love another person while rejecting his body because it is only the body is in effect to deprive the other of his body, and since that is essential to his existence, to make a dichotomy of body and spirit is to commit a kind of murder. In any event, it is clear that the disembodied mind is not the person that passion grasps; when left to itself, passion never fails to deduce the correct erotic conclusion from its affectionate premises.

Now we have the complete person in view, the mind of the other animating his body. At this point a new flood of theories drowns the facts. There are theories that describe the love of another as the love of myself in the other, or the other in myself, or as my reflection in the other, or the other in me, or as the self-adulation of each for himself accompanied by hopes that there is another in a corresponding state, and so on. But all of these theories fail signally to describe anything remotely like the passionate consciousness of the lover, and instead substitute a notion of what supposedly *must* be the case. The "must" derives its force from an *a priori* notion of what the person or his mind is. A person must be a Leibnizian monad, locked within itself, self-sufficient, watching only sensory replicas of something that seems to be going on outside. Thus, according to these theories, there is nothing but a series of self-generated images thrown on opaque shades, and a rapid and complex shifting of images and self-perceptions by which I systematically delude myself into supposing that I love and apprehend another, when in fact I am only loving myself. If the mind is not a monad, then of course none of this needs to be the case. And the evidence that the mind is not a self-enclosed substance, but is in fact and in principle open to the world, a world that at the very least includes others, is as conclusive as any such matter can be. Since a full discussion would take us too far afield, we shall here simply refer to our discussion of existence in Part I. Curiously enough, though, the monadic theory does describe something, though hardly what its authors suppose. For, according to a good deal of psychiatric evidence, the sense of the other can in fact be radically diminished or perhaps even lost, and the resulting narcissism can be carried to a psychotic state in which others become shadowy and also oneself. This is a morbid extreme, however, and it is not capable of grounding any primordial phenomenon.

Let us return to phenomena that are not so complicated as these theories suggest, and are certainly a good deal more interesting. The lover loves the beloved. The loved one can, for certain theoretical purposes, be analyzed into a mind and a body. But a mind without its body is what medieval theology called an angel, certainly not the object of passion; and a body without its soul is dead. Clearly, then, the person who is loved is not a discrete mind or a discrete body; nor is it made up of mind plus body, since one thing can be added to another only when each is distinct. The truth, obvious to passion, is that passion grasps the other as a unique existent living being. That single being is not a synthesis of anything, since we can synthesize only what has been ripped apart by analysis. Passion *grasps* the other as single. We use the term "grasp" to indicate both "understanding" and an actual "taking," as in the caress and the embrace. The translators of the King James Version referred to loving a woman as "knowing" her. Even legal terminology uses the phrase "sexual knowledge." For some epistemologists, this is scandalous confusion. But lovers are unembarrassed by theories and proceed just as if they didn't exist at all. They know perfectly well that the best way to grasp an existing living person is to *grasp* that existing living person, and that such a grasp is at once an existential fusion and the most perfect knowledge one could possibly have of that other living existing person. For just as the mind of one person is not separable from his body, but exists in it and is one with it, so, when two living bodies are united in an embrace, their minds embrace too. Love accomplishes quite directly what the monadic theories declare to be impossible, the existential conjunction of two into one.

When the lover is passionate, he is his passion. If the passion finds its proper object, the other person, the whole lover is complete or satisfied. For as I stipulated before, I am not talking about love as a sideline, but as a passion; that is, as it expresses the totality of the lover's existence. If the totality of the passionate lover's existence is satisfied in the beloved, the two together are a self-sufficient whole. And the lovers themselves repeat to everyone's infinite boredom and jealousy how happy they are, how nothing is now lacking. Aristophanes in Plato's *Symposium* considers such self-sufficient living wholes equal in bliss and power to the gods—so near to the gods, in fact, that out of jealousy the gods cleaved them apart to yield our present separated states.

We now have the simple elements of love. Two living human beings united into a new entity, a whole in which each is an absorbed part. Neither says "I," but both say "we." The "we" of love, as lived within its interior, is therefore a new being, an erotic-spiritual whole totally absorbing the passion, and having no relations to anything outside it. This does not mean that the existing individuals factually do not have external relations; it means that the individuals, insofar as they are actually loving, are related only to one another, and thus phenomenologically constitute a world. The proof of this is to be found again in what everybody knows. If the other does *not* constitute the lover's "world," then the other knows the lover is not sufficiently passionate. For example, to look at one's watch at certain moments is an excellent reason for a quarrel. Or to wonder about tomorrow or about money, to become hungry, to notice defects of grammar or pronunciation in a lover's impassioned words, to take obvious precautions—all of these are instantly noticed by the lovers themselves as constituting not essential aspects of love, but rather signs of its enfeeblement and incipient dissolution. In the same way, to look *at* the other, to examine, inspect, or stare at the other, indicates not lived subjective passion, but rather an objectifying, spectatorial mode of consciousness radically incompatible with love. It is equivalent to hostility and is a dissolution of the interiority of the "we." That "we," as an existing world, has only itself for its own primary content. But it is also the organizing center for a reabsorption of the external world, which now is no longer their world, or my world, but our world.

The world of lovers is a phenomenological whole, lived from within, having its own unique categorical structure. Ludwig Binswanger [1] has examined features of this world in some detail, its unique spatiality and temporality. Contributions can also be found in the work of Jaspers, Buber, Scheler, and others. Let us briefly examine first what a world in general is, then examine some salient features of the world of love, and finally compare the world of love with the worlds of everyday

---

[1] *Grundformen und Erkenntnis menschlichen Daseins* (Zurich, 1942).

common sense and science. Only then can we adjudicate the claims made by lovers, by common sense, and by partisans of science.

To begin with, grant that "being" names what is as it is *in itself*. So taken, being is not yet a world for anything or anyone. It becomes a "world" only when some being lives in it, whereupon it is the world for that being. Or rather a part of being takes on the aspect of world insofar as it is pertinent to the life of a living being. The life of the living being then constitutes or discloses a part of being as its world; without becoming pertinent to that living perspective, being remains inaccessible. Since the world, so understood, is being as it is for life, it is at one and the same time illimitable, an unending horizon of possible disclosures, and yet also finite in its own kind, since the life to which it is correlative is limited in its own kind. A world looks very much like one of Spinoza's attributes of substance, which represents the infinity of substance under a limited perspective. And even in common speech we refer to the various worlds of men, those of the banker, the thief, the musician, the politician. Such worlds are not, of course, things or entities, but open horizons within which certain kinds of entities are disclosed.

If a world in general is some such thing as this, what are the worlds of love, of common sense, and of science? Now we must be careful not to describe any of these worlds from a point of view alien to it. We are interested in a world solely as it is to those who live in it. I have already mentioned a few features of the world of love. The lovers must first enact the fundamental organizing intentionality; that is, they must disclose themselves to one another as lovers. Within this mode of existence, we find that each is exclusively and exhaustively taken up with the other; together they constitute a world. If either is not wholly engrossed with the other, then his attention is wandering and we have a case of the absence of love, not its presence. The world for the lovers is then purely and simply themselves. It is the pure we, wholly and completely grasped in the act of love itself. Such a union furnishes us with exactly what we were initially looking for. It is, so long as it lasts, an instance of that ontological finality that we defined as the absolute. It is in and for itself. It has, in itself, no essential or internal relations to anything else, and is therefore inherently and essentially independent of any other existent thing; it is the actual completion of each I by its transformation into a we, a final value that could not be enhanced by the addition of anything else. It is absolute in every sense. It is therefore with literal accuracy that lovers use metaphysical language, the language of eternity, divinity, and the absolute, to characterize what has happened. For divinity is simply another name for the perfect, the absolute, the final.

The world of common sense, on the other hand, is not organized by love, but rather, as Heidegger says, by care or concern. It is structured by the intention of practical action, of utility, of threats and menaces, and by the forgetfulness of death. The subjective pole is not a we, nor is it an I; it is rather *they,* the anonymous everyone in each individual. This is the public world with its instrumentalities, pragmatic through and through. Its attention is focused on tomorrow; its interest is in what can be done with something, or what it can do for or to us. A major portion of *Sein und Zeit* is devoted to the analysis of this world.

The world of science is fundamentally the world of things, and of persons treated as things. It is the world of the standard and objective observer who transforms other subjectivities into quasi objectives or things. For love you are a you only to a me; and in that mutual correlation or mutual disclosure both of us are involved. We speak to one another, not at or about one another. Hence we are not objective or impartial spectators of one another, but rather mutual involvements. The objective observer, on the other hand, is not involved with his objects; he talks about them but not to them. As an objective observer, he must transform every you into an it. The world of such an observer is constituted of objectivities, things and events, observed in their thinglike relations to one another.

After this brief sketch we can now look at the transformations that the meaning of "love" undergoes as it passes from one world to the other. Love itself supposes that it lives in its own eternity, that the lovers were eternally destined for one another, that they perfectly grasp one another, that their love is the fulfillment of their existence. Common sense, however, takes all this as nonsense. For insofar as the world of common sense is organized and categorically determined by the intentionality of care and concern, it sees everything in the light of what it can do with it, what is going to happen, what is coming next. Again, as Heidegger has made clear, this restlessness is the ontological ground for such an existent's experience of time. For if our immediate experience of time is a consciousness of the not yet, the now, and the no longer, not as isolated and separable parts, but as they mutually affect one another, time is nothing but the form of the tension involved in care. From such a point of view, both the finality of anything absolute and the lived eternity of love undergo a radical reinterpretation. Within the world of care, what could eternity be but an arrest in a static present? And this is but another name for endless boredom and frustration. The static or unchanging is the very definition of death within the horizon of concern.

Within the objective world of science, the eternity of love undergoes an even more radical alteration. For the only objective equivalent of eternity is the atemporal and dateless truth of mathematics or any logical proposition. Or, as empirical science sees it, nothing at all within objective experience is absolute: if it were, if it were utterly wrapped up in itself, it would by that very fact render itself inaccessible to any objective observation.

But the eternity, the truth, the axiological and ontological finality of love are wholly untouched by these considerations. Most clearly, when lovers say they exist in eternity, they do not mean that they find their love an unchanging or static boredom; nor could they possibly mean that they have in the very act of love become dateless abstractions. But "eternity" has many meanings, and it could not have the same sense within the categorical structure of the world of love as it has for either the common world of daily life or the abstract world of mathematics. Its sense is equivalent to what Kierkegaard and Jaspers call the "fulfilled moment" and Nietzsche, the "Great Noontide." If an event contains no internal tension toward what is external to it, toward past or future—if, in other words, it is complete and lives purely within its own actuality—then, from within, it is not temporal. It is not tortured by what was and what is about to be, and if the past and future have any place in it at all, they are subsumed into the present of the loving we. This ontologically complete present can carry no date, has neither beginning nor end, is not serially ordered within time. It simply eternally is. To love is to recur to this eternity. Now if such is the internal sense, structure, or essence of love, its existence must be the existence of this essence and not something else. Eternity, then, exists when love exists. And if causes must be adequate to their effects, there can be no temporal or finite causes adequate to this infinite absolute; the infinite absolute itself is therefore the immanent "cause," present in this moment.

What about the knowledge lovers have of one another? In the world of care, one knows something in the world when one knows how it works, what one can do with it, what is coming next. In science, insofar as science is pragmatic, the same point of view obtains, though now systematically and with the desideratum of a general law and its appropriate evidence. Or knowledge is taken to be demonstrative, as in mathematics. Above all, knowledge for the sciences must be publicly verifiable. It presupposes a standard observer, it aims at a general law, and it wants to predict what will happen. No wonder that the knowledge claimed by lovers is regarded as perhaps the most degenerate form of knowledge possible. It is "mere" feeling. Instead of being a repeatable event for any competent standard observer, love is radically unrepeatable, cannot be produced at will, is never twice the same, and far from being accessible to a standard observer, immediately shrivels as soon as any observer is present. Nor is the knowledge one lover has of another generalizable into a law, in spite of the Lotharios' back-room boasts of the unfailing success of their well-tested techniques and methods. All this spurious knowledge can be told only to a stranger, not to the beloved; for nothing could be more insulting or could wither love more quickly than to find oneself the object of another's supposedly general and objective techniques, which are thought to have worked so often before that there is a reasonable expectation that they will work now.

The knowledge of lovers, then, is identical with their own unique union, is direct and intuitive, discloses only the interiority of the we of love, is not the ground for any prediction, is not hypothetical or general, least of all is inferential, but possesses its object, the we, in person.

Correspondingly, communication within the world of love is radically different from communication in the worlds of common sense and science. Communication now reverts back to its primordial sense of communion. As I mentioned earlier, lovers have only one thing to say, and that is simply "I love you." The rest is nothing but giggling and babbling, nothing useful or informative. Each is related to the other in the form of a gift, not, as in the world of everyday, in the form of utility. Lovers therefore studiously avoid giving one another useful gifts like vacuum cleaners and snow shovels. The objective gift is typically flowers or jewelry; subjectively or essentially, it is themselves. Within the world of common sense, where utility and concern preside, conversation alternates between the amusing and the useful; and in science, where all the standard observers must cooperate, we achieve something altogether different, exchanges of information that may be neither amusing nor useful.

Lovers within their universe declare that they have always known one another. This again is literally true, provided we understand what it means. For if each of the two is characterized by passion through and through—that is, if the passions *are* the individuals, and the individuals are their passions—then, since the passions or the individuals are indeed individual and determinate and not abstract or general, each passion is a determinate passion for a determinate other. No proper lover would ever tell his beloved that he or she was merely one example of an indefinite number of others who would fulfill the same function. And if anyone did say so, it would merely indicate the generalized and abstract character of the person himself. Consequently, the passion is itself a *prefiguration* of the determinate individual who will complete it; and since the person is his passion, it is the literal truth that both lovers always did know each other. Neither may have known the name of the other, but then the name isn't the proper object of their passion. Common sense and empirical science observe that the individuals who have become lovers met only the day before yesterday. True enough, and not contradictory of the preknowledge of the lovers themselves.

In sum, the world of lovers is a world where lovers, as lovers, grasp each other completely, form a we that is complete, final, and absolute within itself and for itself; it has no internal connections with anything else; it is actual yet unaffected by the tensions of time, care, and the inherent split between subject and object characteristic of the world of the observer. It has nothing to do with general laws, either scientific or ethical. Each lover knows the other in the very depth of their intimacy. No generalization follows. No prediction is possible, since prediction itself already envisages another moment, a future, or similar cases, all of which are excluded in principle from love. Ethical laws are suspended. Neither has rights or obligations to the other, for they are not two egos related to one another by a general law; they are a single we. If morality is characterized by imperatives and duties, all love is in principle immoral. There is an ancient Christian motto: Love (i.e., God) and do what thou wilt. Kierkegaard in a similar vein disengaged a moment of authenticity that was the "teleological suspension of the ethical," and Nietzsche regarded *Übermensch* as "beyond good and evil." Categorical imperatives, duties, protective laws, rights, and claims, all belong to the sphere of strangers who must live together without loving one another. When duties are invoked, one can be categorically certain that love has ceased.

Now in general, I believe it is not difficult to see the source of our suspicions of erotic claims. Internally, as the event is lived in and for itself, it is a participation in the absolute; only the vocabulary derived from metaphysics or its equivalent, religion, is adequate to characterize it in essential terms. But no sooner have we finished with this than we observe the contrary:

the lovers fall out of love, tomorrow comes, the perfect knowledge is shown to be ignorant of other aspects of the individual who has become lover, and so on. It was, we come to believe, nothing but delusion. Common sense and its sophisticated development, science, take over, and the whole dream fades. To be wise is to discredit the poets of love. All this lasts until the next affair, at which point common sense and science are promptly forgotten.

Still, though love may come and go, the claims of the lovers are not merely true in their own sense, but also prior to those of common sense and science. The world of erotic-romantic love is, as poetry assures us, "out of this world." I have tried to characterize the internal sense in which this is literally true. But if we examine love externally, it seems to be very much *in* this world. Externally considered, there is nothing metaphysical involved in the matter at all. The lovers are not gods, but very peculiar people, with distinctive ears, warts, sizes, and shapes. They were born at assignable places and times. They met in a certain café on a certain date. They have definite ages and sexes. They must eat, sleep, work, and all this follows the clock ticking on the wall, not eternity. They fall ill from discoverable causes, and are cured by specific remedies. Further, they fall out of love, and eventually they die. Where is the divinity or the absolute in all of this?

But before we become overly impressed with these considerations, let us examine precisely what sort of information they yield. In the first place, the sole causes for love that science or common sense can supply are not causes at all, but merely negative or permissive conditions. If the individuals had not been born, then indeed they could not have fallen in love. But they could also have been born and not fallen in love at all; they might have been utterly indifferent to or hated one another. They must have met somewhere and at some time, or again they could not have fallen in love; but the time and place of meeting could hardly guarantee the emergence of love itself. They must eat, sleep, and work, all to mechanical clock time. These things keep them alive; but they could be alive without being in love. All of these conditions must concur if love is to occur, but their concurrence assures only the possibility of love. The reason these finite conditions can assure only the possibility of the event and not its occurrence is that, of necessity, there is one factor that any empirical consideration must omit, and that is, as we saw earlier, the absolute factor that is the interior structure of the event itself. The event of love, then, is *positively* characterized by absolute terms; those terms are significant only within the event, and cannot be made significant to any external observation. Hence, from the point of view of external observation, armed with nothing but finite conditions and permissive factors, love invariably appears, if it appears at all, as an emergence, or a miracle. The point of view of external observation determines the class of factors accessible to it, and these are, not surprisingly, external factors. They are the contingencies and accidents of the event, which do not and cannot of themselves account for the event, but supply only the conditions that permit it to occur. Externally considered, therefore, they are and must be insufficient to the event that is supposed to arise "from" them. This remains unnoticed by the external and objective observer, since by his very externality and objectivity he is excluded from the interiority of the event. And so the objective observer grasps of love only that which is empirically certifiable: gestures, words, smiles, and external movements. Or, if he is a psychologist, he lumps the whole thing under the rubric "emotion," which again is characterized in quasi-objective terms; the inner structure of emotion remains *terra incognita*. Love, however, is not an emotion, but an ontological event, and it is most accurately characterized not in psychological but in ontological terms. Emotions may or must be felt for it; but what they are felt for is an event, not emotions themselves. For while the emotions as psychological events have their seat in the individual minds involved, this man having his emotions and that woman hers, love is an event involving two persons, the creation of a we. The we is not divisible into two individuals, each of which is a we; the individuals in themselves are simply I's.

The inherent externality of objective observation is further seen in what such observations end up with: the synthetic *a posteriori* proposition. If a proposition is analytic—that is, if there is an essential and necessary connection between its subject and its predicate—then it is regarded as merely tautological and not descriptive of any empirical fact. The only empirical facts, the theory runs, are those in which the predicate is not essentially related to its subject; that is, is related to it contingently or accidentally. Fact therefore is defined by the empirical approach as the contingent and accidental; and this is all that pure empiricism has any right to note or codify. But lovers claim that they are not related to each other contingently or accidentally, but by eternal necessity. They are essentially related to one another; they internally constitute one another in a structural way that must remain inaccessible to any empirical method, whether it be the worldly wisdom of common sense or the analytical methods of science.

My conclusion, then, is that what is externally observed is the accidents and negative or permissive conditions of love, and not its essence or its ultimate formal cause, which is the absolute itself. Its essence is accessible only to the reflective powers of the lovers themselves from the interiority of love and not to anything outside themselves.

Looking at the matter from the point of view of lovers, we can notice how the world of love absorbs the other worlds even when those other worlds reject it. This establishes the *priority* of the world of love over those of common sense and science. If love is out of this world, how does it look back upon the world it is out of? The answer is disappointingly simple: *Love loves it.* What therefore is from the point of view of worldly wisdom accidental and contingent and merely negative, all the externalities of the event, is now from the point of view of the lovers reabsorbed and changed from the accidental to the essential. Hence, whereas dates, times, places, personal oddities, and individualities are indeed the accidental conditions of love, from the point of view of the lovers they now are absolute, essential, and absorbed within the interiority of the we. The absorption takes the form of a celebration: they return to the café where they first met, they celebrate the date and time of their meeting by an anniversary; they remember each other's birthdays, and to the disgust of the external observer they find the peculiarities and even the deformities of the other to be just right. The accidental is transformed into the essential, and the whole affair becomes unthinkable in any other terms than those in which it in fact occurred.

The absorption of nature is quite general. It amounts to what Hegel regarded as the sanctification of nature. Instead of external compulsions and necessities, nature, now absorbed and alien to an objective point of view, is seen to be *our* nature. In short, the lovers now reaffirm their nature, do not struggle against it, and in affirming it as their own and following it they find their freedom. St. Augustine said that love was to the soul what gravity was to heavy bodies. The lover in loving is doing nothing but gladly following his natural bent. And the matter is extended in poetry, where the lyric passes from the beloved to the whole of nature, with all its conspicuous features: the sun and the famous moon, always the birds and bees, flowers, brooks, and the rest of the furniture of romantic poetry. In thus reabsorbing the accidental conditions of love into the essence of it in the form of a free celebration, the lovers now live in the freedom of self-affirmation; their world therefore is that of freedom and not that of external compulsion. How can one be compelled to do what one wants to do?

Even the moral laws, categorical imperatives, and duties that initially present themselves as superior in validity to a love that those laws interpret as mere subjective impulse, hence unreliable and suspect as a guide, or even, as in Kant, of no moral dignity whatsoever, even those laws that condemn love are not themselves condemned in return. They are now regarded by the lovers as making only a single commandment: to love. The helplessness of rational laws commanding love—that is, commanding what is not within their power to command—is ignored; the lovers find that in fact their love is the intended purport of the laws, and within their love the laws disappear as commandments and emerge as prophecies. "Thou shalt not bear false witness" becomes "Love, and thou canst not then be false in thy witnessing or anything else."

The moral, intellectual, and ontological priority of the world of love, then, rests upon its fulfillment of what the other worlds only prepare. And indeed, if there is an absolute content within the world of love, it should not be surprising that this absolute is prior to anything relative and finite, that the relative and finite cannot be understood or justified without reference to something absolute and infinite. The external, the partial, the negative, the contingent have in themselves no sense whatsoever, as Hegel argued at length. Whatever sense they can be said to have can be found only when they are put in their proper place, and that proper place is within an absolute whole. Metaphysics is precisely this pursuit of an absolute finality. I have been arguing that this finality is present in the interiority of love, that it is not present for any external or objective point of view, that the external and objective can be absorbed by the interior and absolute, but not vice versa, and that, finally, philosophies of experience might profitably study other experiences than those of sense data and instruments. If philosophy has any role at all, it must be to adjudicate fairly the claims of various modes of experience. It must, as Plato said, envisage all time and all existence. One mode of experience that we must reckon with and from which all of time and all existence can clearly be seen, more clearly perhaps than from any other, is erotic and romantic love.

6

Intersubjective Time

TIME IS NOW a central theme of philosophy. After many centuries of bedazzlement by the eternal, by the *a prioris* conditioning everything, by insight into "necessary structures" suggesting even an ethics of insight that urged us to emerge from the cave of this world and see the eternal sun himself, or to pursue the blessedness of comprehending oneself and whatever existed *sub specie aeternitatis,* it seems the spell has been broken. It is almost now as if the eternal, the *a priori,* and the necessary were no longer considered understandable, or, which is the same, were affirmed by faith, or perhaps worse, were considered inseparable from the forms of the languages we speak or the way we habitually view the world here in our corner of it, or even as simple endurance. But be that as it may, unquestionably the eternal has for the moment lost its power, and if anything is distinctive of modern philosophy, it is a preoccupation with the temporal, with all that used to be taken for granted or loathed or missed altogether by the predominant tendency of *philosophia perennis.* I should date the conspicuous turning point at Hegel; but in any event, time, becoming, existence, life, and history have been the preoccupations of a sequence of distinguished recent thinkers: Nietzsche, Dilthey, Bergson, Croce, Whitehead, Heidegger, and Professor Charles Hartshorne, to whom this chapter owes much.

But perhaps something should be said to support the contention that time is a characteristically modern theme; for on the face of it, nothing could seem more extravagant. At the beginning of Western philosophy, was not time defined: the moving image of eternity, or the number of motion? Newton conceived time and space as uniform and absolute receptacles, the sensorium of God, within which movement occurred; Kant conceived them as pure forms of *our* sensibility, making individual intuition possible. For Schopenhauer they became the principles of individuation. For Husserl time was one of the most general formal structures of consciousness. But what is striking in these views is that the more time is conceived as pure, formal, *a priori,* the more it seems to resemble eternity itself; we finally end grasping time in its pure essence and as a whole only to see *another* time appear, that which is pertinent to *real* movement, *real* becoming, a time that itself "moves" — the time of the finite world. But what is the form of this new time? And no sooner is it defined than it too takes its place in the heaven of pure form, only to generate its opposite, a newer time, temporalization, or whatever, which when it is defined will no doubt generate still another time, a more authentic time, and on we go again. Time has always been conceived somehow, and yet has it?

This paradox, I am convinced, is irremediable on its own plane. What I shall attempt here therefore is not to supply a new formal definition of time, but rather to consider the context in which the paradox of definition arises. My general contentions are that time is comprehensible only in an ontological context that can both distinguish and relate eternal timeless essence and contingent existence; that time names nothing but the mode of being of contingent existents; that there are as many "kinds" of time as there are types of existence; that the more appropriately *our* existence is comprehended, the more singular and less amenable to typification it is; and that in these subjective senses time is not comprehended through any abstractive or conceptualizing reason, but through modes of experience that are themselves as contingent, existential, singular, and diverse as the subjective existence of which they are aware.

First of all, time and its contrary, eternity, are not fundamental categories. To suppose that there is a single ultimate medium or receptacle called "time," within which we and all the world happen to find ourselves, and which carries us like a boat on some stream, against or with our will, toward a final moment when we either vanish altogether or emerge out of that stream into another realm called "eternity," is to turn everything significant about the whole existent scene into an abstract absurdity. And the point of the absurdity has nothing to do with the place to which we assign that single formal medium of time, whether in pure consciousness as with Husserl, or in sensibility as with Kant, or in the "sensorium of God" as with Newton, or simply in some ultimately irreducible fact of nature, a rocking of the receptacle, as with Plato. For in all cases we end with the notion that we "happen" to be "in" time; time is just there, like some monstrous fatality into which we and our lives have fallen by accident; and then the ethical problem seems to be what attitude we are to take toward this fatality: welcome it or regret it and seek blessedness by lifting the intellectual eye toward pure being, toward eternal substance. Life is seen as a fever and the philosopher as the physician who demonstrates his wisdom by prescribing means of ridding ourselves of it as soon as possible—by an *ascesis* of the will as in Schopenhauer, by the cultivation of insight into eternal being as with Plato, or by the intellectual love of eternal substance as with Spinoza.

But time and eternity are themselves nonentities. Both serve to characterize what genuinely is, but they are not entities themselves. They say something about what is, but are not beings; hence at the start we should avoid all ideas of media, frameworks, *a priori* "conditions," "forms" or any variant of them, streams, weaving looms, consuming fires, fatalities, and so on. Time is nothing but a synonym for the mode of being of existents, and that mode of being is not itself another being. Now, we can mean many things, or think a variety of kinds of thing: events, material substances, persons, political states, the "whole of nature," the "cosmos," God, laws of mathematics and physical nature, and many more. Each of these can be more or less adequately defined, well enough at least for purposes of identification or further inquiry. And each sort of thing we can mean has, strictly correlative to its meant definition, its own characteristic way of being. Its mode of being is that way in which it *must* be if it is to be at all. This general point can be seen by taking some extreme examples. It is not possible for numbers to be events. We can count events, and thereby number them, but the number at which we arrive is not itself a temporal event. Numerical ratios and formulas are thus atemporal in themselves, although it is obvious that temporal events may illustrate them temporally. And so it is absurd to date numerical formulas, although these formulas may describe events that can be dated. Similarly, it is impossible for events to be atemporal or eternal. To be an event is to occur, and without an occurrence there can be no event; but nothing occurs except temporally. It is similarly not possible for a symphony to be in an instant: its *form* may be apprehended nontemporally, and Mozart claimed to have seen whole works in an instant; but what is then apprehended is a *form* of that whose own being is in performance. Many paintings, on the other hand, are made to be apprehended finally in one apprehension; we may first have to explore them, but they are made for a nonsequential final apprehension.

Not everything, then, has such a nature that it must display itself or must be in time; and whether things must be in time if they are to be at all or cannot possibly be in time is a strict correlate of what they are. Time therefore is no medium in which certain things find themselves existing by chance. It is not an accident that life "falls" into time—as though it could be lived otherwise! If we wish an answer to the question why some things are "in" time, or how they must display themselves in time, or why others are "in" eternity, we should examine what they are, for what they are strictly determines the mode of being open to them.

But this is itself preliminary. The next step is to reexamine the "in" when we say we are "in" time. For obviously we aren't really "in" any such thing any more than we are "in" existence. We exist, which is not the same as "being in existence," as though there were some prior thing called either time or existence into which we were thrown. We exist, and other things exist together. Hence there is neither a time nor existence into which we are thrown as into a preexistent medium, but rather we exist together, and time names the distinctive mode in which we exist, a mode that is strictly correlative to what we are. What, then, *are* we, and what modes of being are open to us? For "we exist" is a statement that needs its own proper comprehension. The truth is that if this were all there were to be said, we would have characterized our existences in the worst possible way. To say of a man that he exists is to say the least about his being, and is commonly understood to mean that he is barely alive, perhaps under an oxygen tent. The mode of being thereby expressed is the lowest biological plane on which he can be said to be living at all. It is to be hoped there are other modes of being than this; and each mode must correspondingly modulate time. The time of being under an oxygen tent bears the same relation to the time of decisive personal events as the gasping, wheezing existence under the tent bears to the full flowering of life. To exist under an oxygen tent is not to have the time of one's life.

From this point of view, nothing could be more sterile than the abstractive conception of a single flowing medium within which everything seems to be carried. Such an abstraction can be made, and its making is easy and spontaneous; we simply restrict our attention to that which all existents have in common, and that is changing existence. The sterility of such an abstraction results from the very process by which it was generated; we have by thought reversed that whole ontological development through which bare spatio-temporal events, bare physical things, have developed to become living organisms, and finally organisms that are not merely living, but living consciously and freely, with memory, hope, histories, and destinies—in short, living human persons and historical communities. That single uniform abstractive time is useful for certain specific purposes, mostly of a practical order; but it is utterly useless for characterizing the time that most specifically describes our lived experience. It provides a reference point common to both history and the stars, so that history can be dated in cosmic time; but historical time suffers by the reduction, and such a lowest common denominator has so little to do with the lived time of human history that it should be regarded as more irrelevant than relevant, an accidental convenience rather than an appropriate characterization, more false than true.

Corresponding to the conceptualization of time as a single uniform medium in which all things are is the ontology of such a time: the ontology that looks for being *qua* being: that which all existents have in common, the universal categorization of everything just insofar as it is. It matters little for our present purposes whether such an ontology finds its categories clustering around substance or event, thing or process. In either case, being *qua* being aims at the universal. Next, it should be noted that the universal is inherently objective. That which is common to many possible instances, the universal, can be exemplified only by the objective. The objective to us subjects is that which stands independent of us. But we subjects are not independent of ourselves, and the idea "self" expresses this coincidence of each with himself in such a fashion that we cannot be objects to ourselves insofar as we are subjects. If we alter our position with regard to ourselves in order to objectify ourselves, then in that new position we are no longer selves, but others-to-ourselves—objects. And so the subjective is precisely that which is subjectively identical with itself and therefore not an independent object to itself. Hence the subject is inherently a self, and not an other. As I myself, I am only and uniquely myself; I am not another.

Now, while each self shares this I structure with every other self, it is not by virtue of this universal I structure that any self is a self. The universal structure is therefore only accidental, true of every self, but true accidentally and irrelevantly.

But insofar as objects are objects for me, they must be taken as independent of me, existing out there for my experience or imagination or thought. I am not they, I am not in them, I do not project my own subjectivity into them, I do not vicariously share their own subjective point of view; they are essentially, then, as objects, other to my subjectivity. I encounter them only as they can appear or show themselves to me. For me they can be nothing but their appearance to me, since I am not they and have no privileged access to their individuality and subjectivity. For me they *are* their possible appearance. Each object for me is only its function for me, and any other object that functions in the same way is just as good. Hence the very objectivity of the object decides how it can be for me, the subject: its functioning for me, its sharable phenomenal properties. To be an object is then to be essentially substitutable; for I have eliminated the one thing that would single out this object, its subjectivity. Objects are essentially indifferent to the singularity of one another, and are actually related only through substitutable functions. They inherently "universalize" one another into a replaceability of function. An automobile works with this tank of gas, or any other tankful that functions in the same way.

Hence subjects are inherently singular and only accidentally universalizable, and objects for me are inherently universalizable and only accidentally singular. Ontologies that seek the categories of being *qua* being can therefore only accidentally touch the singular subjectivity, and inherently characterize only the objective. Precisely because of their universality they are inherently objective ontologies, and can touch upon the singular I-am-I only by way of objectifying and universalizing it too— that is, radically distorting it. Now the chief examples of objects for us are material things and events, spatially conceived. The time of such ontologies therefore invariably turns out to be the time of some general objective cosmic motion, the stars, the velocity of light, or the frequency of a band of light in the sodium spectrum. It is this cosmic time that is envisaged as a uniform medium, moving equably in some unending cyclical rhythm. I can locate myself in this time only through that radical misinterpretation of myself by which I objectify myself, range myself with other objects as one among them, and thereby become a member of the physical universe by the surrender of my subjectivity.

Cosmic time is arrived at by observing objective continuous motions, selecting one of these as a standard, and making calculations or extrapolations based upon it. But subjective time is apprehended through neither observation nor calculation, but rather through our conscious involvement in experience or life itself, a participative consciousness. Hence the character and texture of that life will determine its appropriate "time." But "life" is no more unambiguous than "time" or "existence." For, first of all, we mean here life as it is lived by the person living it, not as it might be objectively observed by another, and least of all as that which is common to all lives. And life so taken is not the name of some simple, literal, definable "process" or "experience," but is inexhaustible in depth and incomparable in quality from case to case. For again, even if comparisons are possible, it is not by means of any such comparison or generalization that the inherent singularity is touched, existence as it is to the person who exists.

If life so conceived were a continuous circular motion or a uniform rhythmic repetitiveness, then a cosmic clock would measure it appropriately. And while life may at certain extreme phases almost seem to resemble such a uniform rhythm, such phases are experienced as unutterable boredom rather than as life properly so called. Nor should these views be confused with those of Bergson, who likens this lived duration to a snowball rolling downhill, accumulating the past, moving toward a goal yet to be created. The experience of some life conceivably could resemble some such thing, but life need not; and even at best, the analogy itself makes the time in life comparable to a peculiar sort of objective process. Nor am I in search of Husserl's inner time consciousness, with its uniform, essential structure. For such a structure is accessible only to the reflective, phenomenologically reductive consciousness in search of the essence of pure time consciousness, finding such a structure to be a universal form of all inner consciousness. I am in search of the time that inherently characterizes life or existence in its singularity; and by inherently I do not mean universally, but rather most appropriately. And the life to which time is to be appropriate is that of the one who lives it, a singular, *his* life; and that singularity is its "essential" feature. By singularity, I do not mean that the singular life to which I refer is atomically isolated from other lives, as though in a social or existential vacuum. Nor do I mean that the singularity is itself an objective property arrived at by comparison of this life with all other past, present, and future lives, a comparison impossible in principle, and in any case utterly irrelevant to the sense of uniqueness and singularity of which I am speaking. I do mean that the existence in question belongs only to the self that lives it; it is the life of that self which is and knows immediately that it is itself, without objective comparison. I know that I am I and not another not through any inference or induction, but immediately; if I could not know it immediately, I could not be the self that I am.

Now the time of the life of such a self is as discrete as the self and the life whose time it is. The time of my particular self is radically *my* time; and the common phrase "my time" means "my life" and that which is contemporary with it. It begins with my life and ends with it, even though the stars move on. It is modulated by whatever meanings there are in my life, and is not characterized by the radical senselessness of cosmic time. It is oriented and centered upon my present, actual existence, and is lost in the endlessness of cosmic time. Its experience is my experience of my existence, and is properly characterized by whatever regret, nostalgia, joy, projects, hope, or hopelessness there may be in the very texture of my life. And while it is the time of an individual's life as he lives it, that life itself is not definable or isolable in itself, but is inherently intersubjective or *social*.

The "now" that is essential for any sense of time, cosmic or subjective, cannot be located by reason in any universal or cosmic time; and with that failure, all distinction between past, present, and future fails. The "now" must be located in singular experience. This experience is the presence of a subjectivity other to me. In the primordial presence of subjectivity other to me, the now is born. Time is therefore essentially a social event, an aspect of the encounter of two singular subjectivities in the mode "presence" (and not observation or inference). It is our time; I locate my time in our time, the time of singular human intersubjectivity, "communal" historical time. It therefore follows that lived historical time is prior to cosmic time in definition and in experience, and that that uniform, flowing medium in which we find ourselves is rather based upon the observed motions of *things,* abstracted from a prior time, the time of the life of human encounter and action as it is lived and not as it is observed.

Defining "now" rationally within an objective cosmic scheme presents a problem. Without some "now" there is of course neither past nor future, since the past is past only in relation to the present, and the future is the future of the same present. Without the actual present we have only the general, universal serial structure in which any moment is indifferently in its own present, relative to which other moments are past or future. But every past moment is *for itself* present, and not past; and so with every future moment. Hence any moment can be equally regarded as past to another, future to yet another, and present to itself. So which one of all these cosmic nows, ranged in their endless sequence, is *right now?* Which is *really* present?

We have said that time in its formal emptiness is a series of moments each of which is exactly like every other. Any one of these is indifferently past, present, or future. But even to say this is ultimately impossible for reason, for to posit any moment means that the individual moment must be "selected out" provisionally so that the others may then be treated as past or future to it. But precisely how can reason ever select out, even provisionally, any single moment, when so far as it is concerned they must all be formally identical? In its incapacity to posit any single moment as a now, reason is thus equally incapacitated to regard any "other" moment as past or future to it, and the entire sequence of moments, originally thought of as a series, collapses into one moment, the abstract now that is the commonality of all moments, and which cannot differentiate itself into an infinite series of serially related moments. This abstract now into which cosmic serial time collapses for reason is not, of course, the now we are looking for, but is formally equivalent to eternity. This situation usually escapes us, since it does not occur to us that even to think of time as a cosmic serial order is to presuppose some singular moment that serves as the basis for the rest. But it is the singular existing self that directs its reason this way, not that reason itself. And so to "arbitrarily" select one moment as a now requires that reason, equipped only with its definitions, be arbitrarily arrested at that now. What, then, is the *arbitrium* that arbitrates the matter, enables reason to arrest itself provisionally on just this one singular moment, if not the existing, singular subjectivity? In short, reason, together with its objective, cosmic, serial time order, is incapable of sustaining itself, and is therefore derived from another order of consciousness aware of another order of existence. In other words, upon analysis, cosmic time declares of itself that it is posterior, abstracted, and secondary to some other primordial experience.

The grasp of some moment as singular demands a singular act of consciousness by a singular existent. It may be a gesture, a word used in its indexical function, or an act of living attention or experience. The important thing is that the now can be meant or experienced or grasped in any way only by an act, an event that derives its sense from its actual occurrence. It is not the universal meaning of the gesture that can locate the now, but the living gesture itself, the sense of which is inherently determined by its own singular occurrence. Once the actual now has been located, then by transference we can imaginatively designate other instants as possible nows, again by *living* acts of attention or indices pointing to imagined other moments.

Time, then, is meaningful only for a temporal existent, and not for pure, formal reason. Time can never be completely formalized, since it always presupposes one nonformalizable existential act, a singular act of existence to locate some now, in order to confer sense on the supposed abstract differentiation between past, present, and future.

A second point should be considered. The determination of the now, as reference point for past and future nows, by something that exists now, is itself a preliminary characterization.

There is no possible gesture, index, or act of attention that can settle upon anything like a formal now. The now is always the presence not merely of a form, which would be empty, but of *something*. Time is *filled* time; present existence is the present existence *of something*. And what can be present to us? In the first place, we are not present to objects—that is, to nonsubjectivities. Clearly, it is they that are present to us, and their presence is the same as our awareness or experience of them. What can be present to *us?* And who are we to whom they can be present? When this problem is unraveled, I believe we shall have touched the origin of our own primordial grasp of our own time. The problem, it will be noted, has been shifted from some cosmic scheme of pure or formal time, in which we are supposed to find ourselves but in which rather we lose ourselves, to *ourselves,* the living subjects, experiencing "things" as present to us. Out of this living experienced presence we primordially grasp "now" as the most abstract name for our own existing. It is then our own subjectivity that serves as the origin for the actual present now. "Now" names *our* living actuality and what is contemporary to us. But our own isolated self-enwrapped subjectivity, the subjectivity of the *sum* in *cogito ergo sum,* is itself nonexistential. My existence is precisely my encounter with others, with the not-I. But the particular kind of not-I is decisive here. If my existence is my encounter with others, then the kind of others I encounter, live with, act for or against, determines the kind of life I lead; there are levels of myself called into play, and levels of otherness encountered. In short, encounter is not an unambiguous term; it suffers as many modulations of meaning as the term "life" or "existence" itself, and therewith it modulates as many senses of the term "time."

And so, on the very minimal level, we wind our way back to our mere encounter with physical things. We are now not interested in the supposed cosmic time they keep among themselves. We have located our own living subjectivity in encounter as the origin of the now. But the dimension of the subjectivity operative is coordinate with the dimension of the world encountered. One level of encounter is simple sense experience. I look, and the now is filled with what can be seen and nothing more. It is the now of visible things, and of me as simple looker. My subjectivity is that of a perceiver. The future is the future of perceptive experience; the past is that of past lookings. A reflective oyster provided with memory could do as well. Have we at last found a basic time in which all things that exist can be located? Am I now having the time of my life? I think not. But there are difficulties and obscurities.

Where are we to discover our primordial experience of the present? What sort of object can be present to us, present in the fullest and least derived sense—that is, primordially? Is everything equally capable of being present to us, and therefore of defining a present? Are the barest objects of sensation as fully present as other persons? Can moving points of light serve as well as persons to define the present? If we could rid our reflections of bias, what would we say could be most fully present if not other persons? If something is to be present to us fully, can it be just anything at all, some inert and passive lump out there, or must it not rather be *responsive,* something that of itself offers itself to us? If in imagination we try to enter the world of the mere experience of nature, devoid of responsive persons or responsive things, do we not find our sense of being fully present attenuated? And is it not attenuated to the exact degree that we do not experience such things of nature as offering themselves to us, but simply being there? In short, that vast otherness which we encounter in experience seems to become timeless to the degree that it is impersonal and unresponsive to us. We acquire the faces of swamp creatures, almost asleep, or of naturalists so habituated to the world of stars, trees, and animals that they escape human time, the insistence of the present, and live now in the timelessness of nature, time itself regressing to the cycles of the seasons. But, as I have argued, this is not time, but timelessness. Preposterous as it may sound, it seems that we experience the actual present primordially in our experience of other subjectivities—subjectivities, moreover, which are present to us; that is, which present themselves to us, freely, as gifts. The present, then, is in fact a present or gift of one subjectivity to another; it arises primordially in a mutual encounter, the presence of two presences as a present or gift. Is it purely by a happy accident that these terms are so intimately related? Two subjectivities in mutual presence are two subjectivities in love. "Now," then, names the mode of being of love, and, conversely, love is the origin and support of time.

Lived time begins with some uniquely marked event that is a mutual subjective encounter; mutual presence is the event whose occurrence is the present. It is the irruption into mere uniformity of a determinative event; it is the event par excellence, whose time is only accidentally related to that cosmic time of things which is derived from such unique encounters. Such an abrupt event is an origin; it originates a now, in relation to which other times can be fixed as past or future. It is the time of existence, and it is as finite, singular, and discrete as existence itself. It is inherently and not accidentally an encounter in existence; it cannot be abstractly conceived. Such an event, originating human time, is filled time, filled with the other subjectivity. Its dimensions are the dimensions of existence related to that event: categories such as regret, nostalgia, the memory of what has been, encounter, and hope or despair for the future of encounter. All are rooted in the decisive presence, the unique now of existential intersubjective encounter. These formulas, it now should be added, are themselves indices of singular events. Their final sense is therefore given not through themselves, as abstractions, but in our concrete, historical, singular lives. Cratylus finally cannot say what he means; he can only wag his finger.

7

Memory

Preliminary Remarks: The Problem

LET US USE the term "memory" as a collective name for a series of related subjective acts: retention, recollection, and involuntary recall. For whatever the differences among these acts, they have one thing in common: their sense is to deliver immediately to present consciousness something past. That is, they purport to show us what is no more; whether their claim is just or not we shall consider. Moreover, they purport to give it immediately. Memory, therefore, is not inference. Without any form of memory, subjectivity would be confined to a perpetually changing present, not even aware that it was perpetually changing. And so while the present may be all that is (depending on how strictly we use the words "be" and "is"), memory tells us that there once was something else, and delivers it to us. Memory, therefore, is our immediate awareness of past existence; what never existed cannot be remembered. Hence we cannot remember that two and two make four; they make it eternally, their making it is not an event in existence, and therefore their timeless equivalence is not subject to memory. We can, of course, remember *thinking* about it earlier; but then the thing recalled is an act of thinking, and not some nonevent like timeless equivalence. The Platonic "recollection," then, is a repeated bringing to mind in time of that which is not an event, but an eternal form. Memory is the bringing to mind of what was but is no more. Further, if memory gives us the past, it is an accomplishment; if what I remember could not have occurred, I must conclude that I do not remember it, but only imagine I remember it. But imagination and memory are distinct kinds of act. Can they be distinguished internally—that is, by the subject enacting them? We shall consider this later.

And before we go any further, perhaps a word should be said about some conspicuously different modes of memory. Its most immediate and perhaps least questionable mode is *retention*. Within my present perceptual consciousness, I must distinguish two distinct phases: the actual now and what just was. So, if I hear a melody, in the very hearing of it I must distinguish the actual now from the notes just past, or I could hear the melody only as a jangle of notes sounded simultaneously. I do not *recall* the notes just past; they are still within my present hearing, but in the form "just past." Within my present hearing, therefore, there are notes in two different modalities: the actual note now sounding, and those just past. These two modalities are radically distinct; the notes just past are never taken as actually sounding, or I would hear them all together as a chord or dissonance, and not as a melody. And yet they are still within the whole of my present hearing, while retaining their own distinct modes of being. And similarly if

I look at a flag flapping, I *see* it flapping, and do not *infer* that it is flapping. And what I see, in my present act of seeing, is the flag now here but just having been there. To see it only in its immediate instantaneous present would be never to see it flap; to see where it was an instant ago in the same place as where it is now is to see the impossible. And so within any concrete span of perception, we must discern an actual present together with the immediate past, retained within that larger "present" *as past.* Surely some such thing is the phenomenological fact, and hardly disputable.[1] There are in this domain some curious facts touching the span of immediate retention; some evidence suggests that it is subject to rather wide variations. In some drugged states, for example, it may narrow considerably; the marijuana smoker sometimes experiences himself and his world as hanging in a perpetual present, with the immediate past and the immediate future reduced to a minimum. And since much of the "meaning" of things derives from their apprehended past and presumptive future, their perceived significance alters correspondingly. Faces become shapes.

After an event has passed out of immediate retention, it must be recalled in order to be made present. Recollection brings to mind what has passed out of it, and by an effort of will. That effort of will has, for the most part, to be motivated; we recall, for the most part, what we wish or need to recall for present purposes. Recollection therefore is in the service of a volition that directs present action to practical purposes. For such voluntary recall only the barest schema is necessary; in fact, it is hardly more than recalling that something happened, virtually an affair of propositions.

---

[1] See Edmund Husserl, *The Phenomenology of Inner Time Consciousness,* ed. Martin Heidegger, trans. James Churchill (Bloomington: Indiana University Press, 1964).

But to recall that something happened is not exactly to bring that experience itself before the remembering mind. It is more like a letter of credit the mind issues to itself: under other circumstances, in a quieter mood, the event itself would come forth in all its concrete and immediate detail. None of that is necessary for the purposes of recall, and in fact would inhibit the useful function of recollection. Instead of using only so much of the past as is necessary for present practical purposes, the mind would be flooded with the event itself, stopped by that event, engrossed in its own past instead of the urgencies of the present. Bergson has detailed the economics of all this perfectly.[2]

And so one is inclined to regard recollection as a promissory note whose full payment would occur with involuntary memory. Proust, of course, was the master poet of this extraordinary phenomenon, in which under certain conditions, when the will is quieted, some distant experience floods the memory in such concrete and vivid detail that one can observe in it features that escaped one's notice during the actual experience. For during the experience, attention was focused on the practical needs of that past moment; but now, flooded with the experience itself and having no practical interest in it, the mind can virtually "observe" the horizon of the experience and see in it what was not observed at the time. Such experiences carry with them a subjective indubitability; in all its concrete detail, I know that I am not inventing it, any more than I can be inventing the old house whose rooms I am now actually exploring to see what is in them. I never explore in imagination a house I have imagined; I already know its rooms have nothing in them but what I choose to put there. Involuntary recall is memory *par excellence;* if retention is indubitable because it is

---

[2] Henri Bergson, *Matter and Memory* (New York: Doubleday, 1959).

a phase of present perception, involuntary recall is the least questionable form of direct acquaintance with what has once wholly passed out of present mind, or, more precisely, what no longer exists.

If this is the way it seems to subjectivity, perhaps the phenomenological appearances should be reexamined. Perhaps it is all delusion and unverifiable claims; perhaps Russell and others are right in thinking it possible that subjectivity can be created this very instant, already provided with what it calls its "memories," but what in fact are nothing but peculiar images it finds in itself. And indeed, are we not frequently mistaken? Further, is there not something extraordinary in the very idea that something existing now, the subject, should or even could have a direct acquaintance with something that confesses that it is no more? How indeed can that which exists now, myself, have any existent relation with what no longer exists? Surely this strains our sense of the possible, or at least of what is possible according to certain ontologies. But then, perhaps the ontologies according to which nothing of the sort is possible are either profoundly limited or even impossible themselves.

And so the exploration of memory leads immediately to two questions: What is memory as it presents itself—that is, phenomenologically; is any such thing possible? And if it is, then how must ontology be enlarged to make room for it? Only by examining a phenomenon as it presents itself can we decide whether it may be possible. If it may, then any legitimate ontology must make room for it. No one *knows* what being is, what is possible and what is not; being is always over our heads. Both logic and honesty dictate an exploration without prejudice into what manifests itself; and so let us explore.

The Copy Theory

There would be little purpose in surveying all the theories that have ever been suggested, but let us focus our attention on one principal class of theories, one that is very widespread, directly opposed to common sense, and, in my opinion, opposed to the truth as well. This is the famous copy theory of memory, and for a good account of it we turn to William James.[3] In principle, the theory is remarkably simple. Memory is the feeling or belief that a certain complex image, formed in my imagination, resembles the past. The complex image in which I believe has three factors: the *event imaged,* its *reference to the past,* and its reference to *my past.* It is not sufficient simply to form an image; the event must also be located in its past context, and further, it must be thought to be in my own past. Such, I believe, are the basic elements of any copy theory. James adds that the idea of the past itself comes from conceptual extrapolation from the past I directly intuit in the specious present. But whatever the detail, the copy theory will be examined here only insofar as it describes memory as an indirect knowledge of the real past, mediated by images. I believe there are three things wrong with the theory: all three of its distinctive features.

In the first place, when I recall a past event, there is, I believe, no sense in which I can be said to form an image, copy, or representation of anything. I am not objecting here to the somewhat simplified "picture" theory involved, which is subject to qualifications on other grounds, but rather to the logical paradoxes involved in phenomenological copying. This par-

[3] William James, *The Principles of Psychology* (New York, 1890), I, chap. 16.

ticular kind of theory in effect describes what memory is by
first taking its proper place within the mind in order to become aware of some past event, and then slipping outside the
mind altogether in order to look at the real past event and
affirm that the remembered event is indeed a copy of the real
past event! Surely this is not what memory presents itself to be,
nor can it be the truth about memory from any but a very confused alternation of standpoints.

It is certainly not the structure of memory as we enact it. For
if what I remember presents itself to me as a copy of a past
event, then I must have both that past event itself and my copy
of it present to my mind; how otherwise could I affirm that
my memory image is a copy? But in that case, of course, I already have the past event itself present, in person, so to speak,
and what on earth would be the utility of forming a copy of
it? Further, the presence of that past event itself would be the
genuine act of memory, and not the copying of it. What I remember, then, cannot appear to me, the rememberer, as a copy
of the past, but must appear as the past event itself.

Now it is possible, of course, to become aware of one thing
copying, representing, or imaging another; but such cases are
possible only when both the copy and the original are present,
as when I see a picture of the Grand Canyon while standing at
the rim of the canyon itself, so I can see that the one copies
the other. But this is not memory.

There is another sense in which I may have only an image of
the past, and not the past itself, before my remembering mind.
Here I remember something that I *assume* to be a copy of the
past. I simply take it to be a copy, make it into a copy, or declare that it is a copy. But this cannot be the phenomenological
character of memory either, for memory now becomes even
more complicated and ridiculous than before. Here memory
consists in the complex of forming an image of the past, and

then deliberately forming a second image of the past, or conceiving that there is such an image, and then comparing the two, and finding either agreement or disagreement. In the earlier case, we compared an image with the actuality. Now we compare the image with a past constructed to resemble it, a second past that itself can be just one more image of the genuine past, and the whole weary round begins again. In short, if the image is to appear in any form whatsoever as a representation of anything, both it and what it copies must appear; but that implies that eventually the past itself, and not just an image of it, must appear to the remembering mind. If memory does not present itself as grasping images or copies of things, then this cannot be what we mean when we speak of memory.

Let us suppose that this is *not* the phenomenon of memory, but rather a mixture of memory as we experience it and the objective, external truth about it. Let us suppose that unknown to memory itself, the past that we seem to recall is in fact nothing but a copy of the real past. But for whose mind can such a theory be meaningful? If to ours, then we must have at least the idea of a past that is not remembered, but conceived independently of all memory. We must then have at least the idea of the genuine concrete past against which we compare our remembered image of it. And what about this idea of the genuine past? Is it one more copy of the real past, or is it at last the past itself? If the first, we have an infinite regress; if the second, we have simply another name for memory, and the point is granted that somehow we have a direct acquaintance with the past itself and not merely with its copies.

Thus, as far as I can see, there is no way in which the copy theory can be fixed up to make any sense at all. It does not accord with memory as we experience it, and it has no logical coherence as a theory of memory as it might possibly be in truth. It isn't true at all. And the logical absurdities that follow from it are not accidental, I believe, to some particular formulations; they follow from the roots of the conception—from the view, in other words, that memory gives us only indirect or mediated knowledge of the past, and not that past itself.

Now if we turn to the second feature of all copy theories, we encounter some further distressing results. The copy theory says that we are faced with a number of images or copies, some of which we "refer" to the past, and others of which we do not. All the images are of the same genus, essentially products of the imagination, perhaps "traces" left by what we hope was previous experience. No matter; as rememberers we cannot know which are traces and which are not. But we do have the problem of which we shall refer to our past and which we shall not. But the only criteria that the copy theorists can employ to differentiate a memory image from a pure work of the imagination must be some internal present characteristics of the image itself. And so most frequently the criterion employed is that of "vivacity"; the image we are to refer to the past must be of less vivacity than a present perception, so as not to become confused with it, but of greater vivacity than something purely imagined. And so we are faced with the problem of measuring the relative strengths of images in order to know which image is to be called "memory."

But this is of course absurd. First of all, it is obvious that our imaginations are frequently stronger than our memories, and that we rightly show no inclination whatsoever to regard as memory something that we are imagining, however vividly. Nor do we have any inclination to take rather weak memories as imaginations simply because they are weak. I submit that strength and weakness of image have and should have little or nothing to do with which images we are to regard as memories and which imaginations. Second, what reason should we have for regarding a degree of vivacity as a sign of memory in the first place? The *significance* of memory makes it differ from imagination not in degree, but in kind; they belong to radically different genera. Memory is a recapture of what once was; imagination is something constructed in the present. This radical difference of internal significance has no logical or other relation to "degree of vivacity." In short, when we "refer an image" to the past, we must have some logical motivation for our act, or it will appear even to us as the most arbitrary in the world. We are not at liberty to remember whatever we like, or rather to treat as a memory any image we like. The first aspect of the copy theory separates what we remember from the genuine past, relating them only by possible resemblance. This second feature ends by making memory an arbitrary act of positing or referring some images to the past. The image itself is not already past, or we should have to remember it by still another image; it is present, then, and is merely referred to the past. What in an image can cue or motivate such a reference?

Suppose I perform an experiment. I form an image, say that of myself walking about among the craters of the moon. And now I simply "refer" this image to my own past, and accordingly I should find myself "remembering" it. But somehow or other I do not find myself remembering any such thing, and it remains what it is, nothing but an imagination. The more strongly I exert my powers of imagination and of reference, the more I feel myself slipping into hallucination. *That* cannot be what memory is. The dilemma may be stated thus: Either memory is identical with the act of "referring," in which case we have explained nothing, or the two are distinct, in which case the act of referring becomes arbitrary.

The third feature of the copy theory touches on a matter essential to any description of memory, but unfortunately, as it occurs in the context of this theory, it becomes perverted.

James says we refer the image to *our* past. "It must be dated in my past. In other words, I must think that I directly experienced its occurrence. It must have that 'warmth and intimacy' . . . characterizing all experiences 'appropriated' by the thinker as his own." [4] Now this is true enough, so long as we forget that the "appropriation" of an experience as mine is itself, for James and for anyone else holding the copy theory, nothing but a present attribution or feeling, and therefore represents no genuine acquaintance with my genuinely past self. "I must *think* that I directly experienced its occurrence." But what makes me think that I experienced some imaged events and not others? "Warmth and intimacy." Forgetting warmth, let us look at intimacy, for what we remember is more intimately connected with our past than what we imagine, since it indeed *was* a part of our past. What is intimate is mine; and I must recognize that what I remember was indeed my experience once. But it is quite insufficient to assimilate our recognition of our past with a present feeling of intimacy with the imagined event. Thus the entire insight is transformed by the supposition that I need only *think* now that the event was mine, whereas memory claims to *recognize* that it was mine. Again, the alteration is from a theory of memory that credits it to a theory that seeks to describe it purely "psychologically" as a series of present images, all of which is but a "complex representation" of what may or may not have been the truth.

In short, the copy theory must find the remembering mind enclosed within a gallery of present images, embarrassed by its task of choosing which are to be regarded as memories and frustrated by the very *significance* of regarding them as memories. To make the rickety theory work, we must be both within and without our minds at the same time, we must both credit

[4] *Ibid.*, p. 650.

and discredit our only access to the past, and we must be endowed with faculties for measuring quantities of strength, vivacity, warmth, and intimacy, which have, as we have seen, no particular significance anyway.

Now the philosophical motivations for the copy model are not far to seek. What is it but an elaborate device to quiet an epistemological fear: the notorious fallibility of memory? And indeed, if memory is in principle fallible, then we might have to construct some sort of representation theory, to put the real past at one remove from direct knowledge. The copy theory can account for some sort of error, but it is questionable whether it can account for anything else. Error, or what seems to be error, certainly needs to be explained; but it would seem dubious procedure to become so impressed with error that we introduce it as a permanent possibility within any unique mode of awareness. If any unique access to an object is declared fallible in principle, how shall we correct it?

To make memory in principle fallible, and therefore dependent upon external inferences for validation, seems to solve one problem; but of course it merely conceals it under another name. For how are we to validate the very rules of inference by which we are to check our fallible memory? If memory in principle is fallible, then every memory can be wrong, and the past becomes a perfectly gratuitous assumption. Not only is it a gratuitous assumption, but ultimately it is a meaningless one. For if our only knowledge of the past is mediated, or constructed from present materials, by what magic does the mind arrange, rearrange, or interpret ever present data and acts, in order to make them copies, traces, or representations of that which itself never appears? Is it not like some attempt to construct sound out of colors?

We must therefore return to the phenomenon of memory itself, first suspending our epistemological dreads and ontological suppositions, to see whether memory as it presents itself to reflective consciousness is not what common sense supposes it to be, a direct vision of the genuine past, and veridical to the extent that it is clear. We shall then see whether such a description of memory is not perfectly capable of taking care of the erroneous cases as well, and further, whether it may not have important implications for ontology.

Memory as Direct Awareness of the Past

The first thing to be decided about memory is precisely what it is that is remembered. At first glance it might seem that what I remember is a simple past event, the building burning yesterday. And indeed, this is where our explicit attention usually focuses, upon the thing or event remembered. But it is equally clear that in fact I am not simply related to a past burning building, but rather to my past *experience* of the burning building, since if I did not experience it in the past, I certainly could not now remember it—that is, remember myself experiencing it. It is emphatically true that when I remember the past event, my explicit thematic attention is on the past event and not on myself; but reflection discloses that in fact I am also implicitly aware that the event was an object for a past act of experience. However, since that act of experience was intentionally directed upon its object, the burning building, the act of experience itself becomes relatively invisible or transparent, leaving me now simply with the explicit event. That the event I now remember is not simply an independent occurrence but an event as it was experienced is not itself a hypothesis, but a present phenomenological fact.

And of course I remember not only sense experiences, but also any past object, so long as it was the object of some mode of consciousness. Thus I can remember reasoning about mathematical objects, entertaining ideal entities, and so on. I can remember any object whatsoever, so long as it was the object of some past act of consciousness.

Thus the total fact remembered now is a past act of consciousness directed to its own object, wherein the object is explicit and thematic, since the past act of consciousness was itself directed to it intentionally. In other words, I now remember (myself looking at) a burning building. Now this is obviously a *reflexive* conscious act, for insofar as I am now aware of a past awareness of an object, that past object has become accessible to me only through my present awareness of a past awareness. If consciousness were not capable of this reflexivity, memory would be impossible. It should be noticed that this reflexivity is not that of one act of consciousness folded back over another simultaneous or present act of consciousness, but a present act of consciousness reflexive upon a genuinely past act of consciousness, and through that reflex, upon a genuinely past object. It should also be noted that in this view, nothing copies anything else. I am now directly aware not of a copy of the past experience with its object, but of that past experience itself. And even if we extend the analysis to that past experience, it is not the awareness of a copy of its object, but of its object itself. This consideration carries us into the vexing problems of neorealism, critical realism, idealism, and so on, and further discussion is not strictly necessary for our present purposes.[5] For now we are not concerned with the so-called past *physical* object, but solely with its past appearance. A physical thing is not related to its sensory appearances in the same way in which those sensory appearances are related to our memory of them. For in the first case we may suppose that cause and effect need

---

[5] For a fuller analysis, see my *Objectivity: An Essay in Phenomenological Ontology* (Chicago: Quadrangle Books, 1968).

not belong to the same categories, but in the second this is impossible, since we are only trying to recall a past experience as it was at the time, and not its physical causes. It is this content of a past act of awareness that I now try to recover through memory. My first observation, then, is that memory is a reflexive act of awareness wherein a present act of awareness has as its direct and unmediated object a past awareness of some object.

My second observation concerns the *content* of memory. If we turn to the intrinsic character of what it is we are remembering, it is clear, I think, that it does not and cannot contain within itself the predicate "past." It *is* past, of course, but it is past only in relation to my present act of remembering it; and what could it have known of my now? And so what I recall is myself in the past seeing a burning building, but the content, myself seeing a burning building, is in its own present and not at all past with respect to itself. Hence nothing remembered can carry the predicate "past" stamped on its face for easy identification, neither the past experience nor its past object. They are in their own present.

If we should suppose for a moment that the event recalled had as one of its internal properties the fact that it was past, we should find ourselves in the ludicrous position of remembering an event that is past with respect to itself, an event whose very passage was retrospective, which lived for the sole purpose of being remembered, an event that had already occurred at the very moment it was occurring. If then the content recalled is in its own present, and I as I recall it am in my own present, where does the past come in? How do I ever become aware that it is indeed a past event I am now recalling? It is a mistake, I believe, to look for some intrinsic character in the object experienced which will suggest to us that it is past, either its vivacity, its coherence or incoherence with present perceptions, or some other internal part of it such as its inclusion of a calendar page. No characteristics of this sort could conceivably guarantee that the event they characterized must have occurred in the past, or distinguish it from anything imagined. That event is remembered solely by virtue of the fact that I experienced it before; and therefore we must look to the character of the reflexive act of consciousness that brings it forth again. When I am aware that I experienced it before, I then remember it. Otherwise I simply entertain it as an imaginative object.

The essence of memory is therefore located in the relationship between two acts of consciousness, one present and one past; and, descriptively, what more can be said but that I now am simply aware that I was aware of something before? Since, according to my first observation, my thematic attention is on the object of the past experience, and, according to my second observation, this object itself contains nothing of the past in it, I should now say that my awareness of the pastness of my experience of that object is lateral or implicit. Hence the more I turn my attention upon the objective content remembered, the less certain I am that I am remembering and not imagining, since the same object might be given imaginatively. But the more I become aware of the fact that I did actually experience that object, the more certain I am that I am remembering.

Our awareness of the past, then, focuses itself between two acts of consciousness, the present recollecting act and the past recollected act; and while our attention directs itself to the object of that past experience, we have a lateral awareness that it is an object once experienced. The conjunction of past and present occurs within reflexive mind, and is a genuine conjunction of the actual past of consciousness with the actual present of consciousness, and has nothing to do with images, copies, or representations of anything.

The third and most important aspect of memory is one that was noted by James, although I think incorrectly interpreted. It is that when I remember, I invariably remember myself having had an experience. Thus part of the original and immediate deliverance of memory is that some particular event happened to *me*. Obviously, I do not remember an experience that someone else had, or that nobody had. But what interpretation should this receive? And here it should be borne in mind first that when I genuinely remember, I do not *infer* that the past event happened to me, but rather *recognize* that it happened to me. And second, the me to which it happened in the past is not wholly a past me, but also me now, the same me that is now remembering, for it is I now that claim the past experience as my own. Now these simple facts are, I think, rather remarkable. I have the same assurance of them as I have that I am now remembering. But what does it mean for me now to recognize some past experience as mine? Again, the direct deliverance of memory itself makes a claim that I believe cannot be denied or explained away, no matter how complex our hypotheses. And that claim is that on one level, I am numerically identical now and then, that there is only one I that once had some experiences I now recall as mine. The inescapable fact is that they could not be recognized as mine now unless I were the same then and now. Otherwise, they would have belonged to another. It is always the I *now* that says that the past experience belongs to it, not that it once belonged to it. The "mine" therefore indicates the relation that unites past with present.

If the I is identical now and then, it is, of course, atemporal; time has made no bite into it, or differentiated it into passing events. The I is of course related to passing events, or time itself would be an illusion. And it is related to them by its acts of consciousness, which are temporal acts, unrepeatable and separated in time. My present act of remembering is not identical with my past act of experiencing; but the I that experienced the event then and recalls it now must be one and the same, or my past acts would not be mine now.

One further point: We should be careful not to think of the identity of the self as some sort of endurance, as though there were a tube of selfness stretching back through a duration, one end of which looks at the other and notices that they are similar. Similarity presupposes numerical diversity; and what that past similar self experienced would not be mine now, but rather an act of a merely similar self. When I remember some experience as mine, I am not in the least peering down a corridor of the past, noticing various myselves stationed along the way wearing more or less similar clothes. Rather the beginning and end of the tube must be made to coincide, which means of course that there is no tube, but instead sheer identity. The self in its core is therefore atemporal, while its various acts take place in time. Time differentiates only the acts, not the self that does the acting.

Of course, any description involving the word "eternity" has a good chance of being taken for a speculative hypothesis. But our common inner conviction of the eternity of the self is hardly of this order. The conviction of the eternity of the self is found in children, savages, and the sophisticated alike; it can hardly have the status of a theological or metaphysical hypothesis designed to account for rare and subtle matters of whose very existence we have no certain belief. And since such a conviction is not a hypothesis, it cannot be argued away, and remains in spite of all theoretical interpretations or refutations. It is more likely, then, that it is simply uncovered by our own instinctive explorations of consciousness. I have tried to show the possibility of a lateral awareness of our own eternity simply in the phenomenological exploration of the act of memory.

Let us now try to gather together all these observations and see if they form a coherent description of the phenomenon. Our first observation was that memory is reflexive, and that the reflex is within consciousness, not within the objective world. It depends on a consciousness of consciousness. Next we observed that there is a genuine factual difference between past and present acts of consciousness, and that memory is simply the presence of a past act of consciousness to a present act of consciousness, along with the awareness of their factual temporal difference. And third, we found that there is an intrinsic binding together of past and present in the identity of the self that both experienced the past event and now recollects it. Has not the third aspect of the total phenomenon unified the whole into an intelligible scheme? The past event has gone and is no more; but now I have the power of calling it forth, or putting it in my presence. The presence to me now of what is no more is rendered possible by the self that was identically present at both times. There is a genuine gap between the past and the present acts; but to say this is not to say the last word. If it were, how could we recall it? The gap must be bridged by the self that presided over both occasions, the same and identical self. The entire affair occurs within mind, but there it is a genuine event. The past object cannot act physically on a present one; it has gone forever. But it can stand in the *presence* of ourselves now. The presence of the past to the present through memory is thus an actual event, occurring within the whole of being; but it is not a physical event. It is an enacted relationship, with one leg in the present and the other in the past—in the past itself, and not in some present copy of it. Thus memory supplies us with one of the most curious phenomena in the world: the past and nonexistent appearing in person to the present and actual. Nothing like it is to be found in the physical world, and from what has been said, it is clear that no purely physical or physiological mechanism can account for it. For either we must attribute to such a mechanism powers identical to those of the mind, which is of no explanatory help, or we must leave them physical, which means located in their own space and time. But the phenomenon to be accounted for spans the gap. How can a mechanism that is itself located purely in the present render present the real past?

Such, then, I believe, is the phenomenon of memory. And this is all that I have to say positively about it. But there are some objections that may give us pause when we wish to accept the phenomenon of memory as it presents itself.

Two Objections

The first objection is epistemological. If memory is a direct vision of the past itself and not the awareness of an imaginative copy of the past, how is error possible? And yet we have all experienced the difficulty of knowing whether our memories are correct or not. It is the fallibility of memory that has led many thinkers to suppose that we are in principle at one remove from the real past, that we know it solely through the mediation of present images that pretend to copy the past, but which may not live up to their pretensions. About this objection or epistemological worry a few things should be said. In the first place, the choice of example is crucial. If we want to know the structure of memory, we should choose as our example the very clearest case we can find, the freshest recollection of the most immediate past, and not the most obscure case. This should go without saying, but is frequently violated in theory. If I wish to know what desire is, I should not choose some obscure mental act whose character is so indeterminate or indeterminately grasped that I do not even know whether it *is* an instance of desire, and not perhaps emotion, thought, or perception. If we are interested in differentiating the essential structural peculiarities of things, we must select the simplest and clearest cases we can. If I am illustrating a geometrical theorem about a circle, I must draw a figure that is unmistakably a circle, and not an oval or a square or a shape with a meandering outline. Nothing of any theoretical interest can follow from vague and indeterminate instances, except that we do not know what we are talking about. Hence our examination should begin with the clearest and most unmistakable instances of memory, and not with some dim, vague, fleeting phenomena whose character is too unstable to favor any theoretical interpretation. And having before us a clear case, we must then indicate precisely how it may lose its outlines so as to become confused with something else. An ellipse is not a circle, but after having defined their differences, we can indicate how an ellipse that is very nearly circular may be taken for a circle. Memory is most frequently confused with imagination, so that "erroneous memory" is in fact simply imagination, accompanied by the judgment that what is imagined is indeed a past event being remembered. Let us then compare the clearest cases of imagination with the clearest cases of memory.

I now deliberately feign having been in the next room a moment ago. I compare this imagination with my clear memory of having been at this typewriter. Now I cannot, in all honesty, declare that these two acts intrinsically resemble one another in the least, or that their differentiation rests upon external evidence. They would have to be very confused indeed to be mistaken for one another; and the clearer they are, the more clearly they seem to be acts of a radically different order. When I *deliberately* feign an event and attribute it to my past, I know precisely what I am doing. The imaginative surrogate for memory is my own construction, an act of my constructive will forming and holding together voluntarily an image that I then assert by another act of will to be in my past. In the case of memory, I am aware of the past event and of the fact that it is in my past. Now an immediate awareness of a past event as in my past is not at all the same as an awareness of an event combined with a *judgment* that it is in my past. Of this I can assure myself by deliberately judging events to be past, or feigning that they are past, or trying to believe they are past, and comparing such an act with immediate memory. In the case of memory, I have the past event itself given through a lateral awareness that it was an event in my past; in the case of judgment or feigned memory, I have no such lateral awareness, but rather the lateral awareness of a deliberate act of judgment.

In these clear cases there is no doubt whatsoever as to which is memory and which imagination. Memory declares itself to be memory by its own intrinsic character of being precisely an immediate awareness of the past, and imagination declares itself to be imagination by the accompanying awareness that its bogus, memory-like appearance is the product of my own will. If the clear cases are indubitable, we must conclude that memory, to the degree that it is clear, is immediate and indubitable; and that it not only is not but cannot be mistaken for imagination so long as it remains clear. The *structure* of memory, then, consists of an immediate vision of the past; this is an eidetic truth about it. It now follows that any given instance will participate in this indubitability to the degree that it is an instance of memory, and that the instance can of itself exhibit the essential properties that qualify it as memory. Hence to the degree that any act is clearly memory, to that degree it will be an indubitable awareness of the past.

But, as I remarked above, not every act of the mind is an indubitable instance of memory. In fact, there are no acts of the mind that cannot lose their outlines and share in the essential character of some other act, or at least seem to do so when our attention on them becomes distracted, weak, or faltering. And so when the direct lateral awareness of an event in my past weakens, or when my awareness of my own voluntary role in the production of imaginative images weakens or passes unnoticed, then I am no longer sure whether I am remembering or imagining. Hence the data supplied by the reports of children or of psychotics are of most questionable relevance to our problem. To unclear, dreamy, unfocused, or disintegrating minds, nothing at all need be clear. What significance can such data have for minds that are not so distracted? If there is some mind that is too distracted to see that one equals one, does this truth then become in principle doubtful, and do all the intuitive insights of reason become questionable? Must we conclude that we really do not know when we see that one equals one and when we do not? Or that we are actually reasoning about images or copies of the mathematical truth, and not about that truth itself? Or, to take a more relevant example, if someone should adduce a rational error in a very complicated proof, does that invalidate reason when it works on something simple?

If we occasionally do not know whether a given act is memory or imagination, the explanation may be that the act itself is too dim and vague to be clearly classified. But usually the error is not so simple. Usually I genuinely remember something, but add to it certain imaginative contents. There remains a core of genuine memory, dressed up with imaginative additions. But the explanation of this is not difficult. The mind is of course enormously and systematically complex. The act of memory becomes itself the subject of another act of memory, and because the mind is invariably active, soon the original core is overladen with additions from later perceptions, later memories, and later imaginations, all of which are again subject to intermodifications and further complexities. No wonder that we can hardly have much confidence about our memories of a week ago, unless the event was so novel or interesting that it emerges out of the matrix with special clarity. And it is this mishmash that worries us when memory is said to be indubitable. But it is certainly not from such complex and compounded products that we should take our examples, but from the clearest cases possible, such as our memories of a moment ago.

In certain cases, then, it may be difficult if not impossible to distinguish memory from imagination; that is to say, to decide on the basis of internal evidence whether a given act is memory or imagination. But what would be the sense of trying to distinguish the two if memory were nothing but imagination that happened to agree externally with the past? In that case, there would be no utility in even trying to remember, since we would be exercising exactly the same faculty.

The second matter to be noticed in this connection is that the copy theory makes the relation between its "image" and the genuine past purely coincidental. That is, it is accidental to the image whether the past resembles it or not, and no inspection of that image can reveal its correspondence. My own theory makes the past itself *internal* to the act of remembering, given along with the past event itself. Now clearly our sole acquaintance with the past must come through memory. Hence if we relocate ourselves back into our true position, that of minds whose exclusive access to the past is through memory, it turns out that according to the copy theory we are in a rather foolish box. For the past, according to the copy theory, is always external to the act of memory, and therefore, since we are not external to our own minds, we have in principle no access to the past itself or even to the meaning of "past."

It is clear what has happened. The copy theory has intruded into its description of the essence of memory a theory of a method of verification, so that memory becomes a compound of both itself and a method for verifying it. This is absurd in its own right, and futile in the long run, since the method of verifying memory by indirect means also presupposes precisely that validity of memory which is deemed questionable. The end result is that according to the copy theory there need be no past whatsoever, for all memories might be false copies; hence the past itself becomes a gratuitous assumption, bolstered by a series of elaborate arguments about the coherence of experience supposed to result from the assumption of a past. Phenomenologically, however, the past is no assumption, but rather a datum given directly to the mind in some clear cases.

The second objection to the notion that we can directly inspect the past is hard to specify but nonetheless effective in controlling our beliefs. Memory has two aspects: it is a cognitive act claiming to acquaint us with the past, and therefore it must defend such a claim against epistemological objections; but also, since it is an act, it is something that occurs in the universe, something that must therefore defend itself against ontological objections that such an event cannot occur. What, after all, does the phenomenological description of memory ask us to believe? Nothing less than that the mind here and now can establish actual relations to a past that is no more, or that what has passed away forever can be called up and stand in the actual presence of an existing mind now. It therefore maintains that the remembering consciousness can somehow span one of the most fundamental diremptions in our experience, that between the past and present, or between what is no more and what is. Finally, it takes seriously the eternity of the self, finding it not only a phenomenological datum, but precisely that mode of being which might conceivably make possible the union of past and present in memory.

Now all of this is a good deal to believe, and surely one level of our common sense must cry out in protest that this sort of thing is simply impossible. And so once again we find ourselves with a philosophic problem: our own common sense would like to believe that its memory is a direct acquaintance with the past, but it also finds precisely this order of events quite incredible.

I have defended common sense in its first conviction, but I shall now oppose it in its fundamental ontological convictions. It goes without saying that common sense of itself is no touchstone for theoretical truth. At the same time, it has a long and intimate acquaintance with its own nontheoretical activities. We find accordingly that our immediate or naive views of memory, our pretheoretical interpretations of memory, are quite stable, whereas our theory of what the whole thing is about is apt to change with every shift in prevailing views of the nature of the universe. Since the theories of common sense are little but echoes of dominant suppositions, they have little claim upon our attention; but the pretheoretical interpretation of our immediate life, in which common sense has some practice and concern, is more likely to be of interest. Let us try, then, to render explicit the character of the ontology that forces our disbelief in the immediate deliverance of memory, and see whether it is at all credible.

There are, I think, two basic premises of such an ontology,

one having to do with time, the other with causality. The first is an insistence upon the absolute finality of temporal distinctions. Within any specified coordinate scheme, the past is past, and is simply gone. This premise, stated more abstractly, identifies *being* with *present being.* All that is, in any sense, must be existent now. The past does not exist now, and therefore it has no being whatever; and if it has no being, how can I inspect it? It does not exist for inspection. Therefore I am not inspecting it; all I can inspect is a present image of it.

The second premise is that each thing is situated where it is and when it is. Things are dispersed in the media of time and space, each in its own pocket. If one thing is to affect another, its influence must travel through the medium until it touches the thing to be affected. So long as two things remain separated in space or time, they must be indifferent to one another, neither acting upon or knowing the other. In other words, no action at a distance. How then can the remembering mind pretend to jump across the gap of time and cognize directly something that lies in its past? What it cognizes therefore does not lie in its past, but is, again, a present image. Such, then, is one of the ontological reasons for insisting that what I now cognize in memory is nothing but a present image. The phenomenological description, on the contrary, presents us with a most paradoxical situation: the act of remembering is enacted now, by a present mind, but the terminus or object of the act is genuinely in the past. How can the present act and the past object be brought into relationship? Where and when can the relationship be?

Both of these presuppositions should be well examined. They cannot be discussed here with the thoroughness they demand, but enough can be said, I hope, to indicate that there are very solid reasons for rejecting both of them. The first premise reduces itself to a one-dimensional ontology. If indeed being is confined to the present instant, then memory is incredible. Similarly, if nothing is but the eternal, there can be no memory. Memory becomes incredible if being is reduced to any single dimension. The solution lies in conceiving dimensions in being, so that by itself neither the present nor the eternal is the whole of being. I have, then, no intention of declaring that the past is the present, or that the past does not exist at all, or that the past is eternal. All such assertions can be nothing but radical confusions of language and thought. What is the past? What mode of being does it have? Let us look again.

The past does not exist now. It is simply a flat contradiction in terms to say that the past is now existing, for if it were, it would not be past. The past as past is never present, and it is futile to try to imagine it as having some shadow or ghostly existence hovering around the same place it once occupied. How would such a belief differ from the rank superstition that the dead are still living (though also, of course, dead), but simply invisible—or perhaps just *barely* visible to the believer—watching us, and ready to intervene for or against us? Souls may or may not be immortal, but they surely are not immortal in this fashion. Nor does the past still linger in the present, with its own subtle matter and its own mode of efficacy. We cannot collapse the distinction between past and present; they are different, and never shall they be simultaneous.

Nor can we say that the past does not exist at all. As past, it is the subject of true propositions; and just what would such propositions be about if their subject matter had fallen back into pure nothingness? Propositions about the past are certainly not propositions about other propositions in the present, or about our ideas of what the past might be like, but about the past itself. If they are true, their subject matter must have its own determinate mode of being and character. The past must be what true propositions assert it to be; the past therefore has its own distinctive and determinate mode of being.

Is the past then eternal? No, it certainly is not simply an eternal fact, for the event that is now in our past was once present. It was not eternally past, or it never would have happened in the first place. To be sure, it has its fixed and immutable order in the series of events; but such an order simply dates it in the series and does not determine whether the event is occurring or not. It simply determines that the event is before another event in our present and after other events in its past. Thus the past cannot be assimilated without remainder into an eternal serial order. We say, "Caesar crossed the Rubicon"; Caesar's contemporaries said, "Caesar is crossing the Rubicon." The past therefore, insofar as it is past, is not an eternal fact.

The past is not nothing at all, nor is it existent now in the present, nor is it laid up in eternity. All such notions rest upon a conviction that being has no modes, that it is literally reducible to one of its own specifications. And so what mode of being *does* the past have? But is there any authentic puzzle here? There is only bewilderment in conceiving the past if we try to reduce it to something it is not. The past quite simply is past, and that is the end of it. It once was and now it is no longer, hence it is not present. It is what once was, a determinate something; hence it is not nothing. It once was but now is gone; hence at least that fact about it is not eternal. Precisely what further question are we asking about the past which is not answered by its very name? Or has this term also suddenly become meaningless? We must, as Descartes remarked, stop asking questions when we already have something so clear that any further "explanations" would only obscure the object. The problem is not what the past is; that is known as clearly as anything can be known. The problem is in extending the notion of being to include the past. And that problem is not solved by further analysis of the past, but by extensions in imagination and reason to render them adequate to what undoubtedly is.

If this is what the past is, how is it related to the present? How can we, in our present, inspect it? Is not the inspection itself a bond between them? If temporal distinctions are final, then again memory becomes incredible. But of course, as Hegel argues at length, distinctions are never final. Items that are distinguished are also united, not in the same sense in which they are distinguished, but in a higher sense. A distinction is a separation of what is not separated prior to the distinction. Distinction distinguishes within a whole, and the very sense of distinction implies the connectedness of what is being distinguished. In other words, the sense of a distinction can never be to sunder the distinguished aspects into unrelated universes. Thus the past is past and the present is present, and on this level neither is ever simultaneous with the other. On the other hand, what is it that is being so differentiated? Within what whole are these moments distinct? That whole or unity cannot be characterized by terms appropriate to the level at which the distinctions are found; that unity therefore is itself neither exclusively in the past nor exclusively in the present. Nor is it unrelated to past and present, since it is precisely the whole of such moments. The traditional name for such a unity is, of course, "eternity."

The example of hearing a melody is used so frequently that I hesitate to use it once again; but it is clear and decisive. The notes, we recall, are not heard atomically and wholly separated from one another, nor are they heard simultaneously. They are heard both together and separated, in their serial order, so that they form a whole. Their serial order is a distinction within the whole, and that whole is not itself a member of that series. Now hearing the whole melody is itself an event within a larger whole. But we are not here talking about the event of hearing the melody, which is a psychological act, but about the heard melody itself, and that melody is a whole of the same order as the whole that comprehends all moments of time.

But external events do not remember themselves. We remember our former acts of consciousness. What is relevant to memory is the eternal being of consciousness, since memory is an act of consciousness. And the eternal dimension of consciousness, which is identical now and then, and which is consciously so identical, we have called the eternal ego or self. In short, while all events strung out in time participate in eternal being, they do not all do so consciously; when such participation does take place consciously, and on the level of intuitive perception and not of hypothetical inference, we arrive at the possibility of memory with its collateral consciousness of the eternity of the self. The notion of eternity, then, is essential not only for any adequate description of objective temporal events, but also for any adequate description of the subjective act of remembering. And it does not cancel temporal distinctions, but rather preserves them in a higher unity.

The second premise of "common-sense" metaphysics whose influence lends an air of extreme paradox to memory is a conviction about causality. Our notions of causality are derived for the most part from science, or what was science until recently, when notions of statistical constants assumed the role. No action can occur at a distance, whether the distance is spatial or temporal. If anything was but is not now, the only way it can act in the present is by means of influence that endures or is transmitted into the present. Thus we feel that "brain traces" are the causes of memory; there must be present modifications of the physical matter of the brain to account for anything now occurring in the mind.

Now whatever the role of the brain is, and we do not wish wholly to forget it, we should also be clear about the categorial question. It is certain that the mind is not related to the object of its consciousness by any causal relation whatever. The conscious subject is related to its object by *presence,* and not by physical influence, touching, or any other mode of causation. When I recall the past, that past event cannot be *acting* on my mind, since indeed it is passed away, which means precisely that it has lost all power of acting. Nor is my consciousness acting upon it. Once an event is past, how can I alter it? In short, that past event is not modified in its own intrinsic character by my becoming aware of it, nor is it acting upon my present consciousness through any effort or influence of its own. It stands in my presence, and presence is not a physical relation. This is true not only of memory, of course, but of any cognitive act. Even in present perception, the external physical stimulus does not act upon my consciousness, but only upon my sensorium. I must become aware of its influence by my own free conscious act, by which I pose it as object. Hence the worry about causation is a monstrous *ignoratio elenchi.* The conscious subject is in no case touched, moved, or physically acted upon by any physical influence, whether it is actually perceiving such a physically existent thing or not. The problem, then, is not to find some peculiar mode of causation by which the past actually acts now on present mind, but to understand the phenomenon of presence itself. And this of course will introduce other and unique categories. For the moment, we can only conclude that an ontology that finds it impossible for the past to be directly present to consciousness rests upon assumptions that themselves need reexamination. Ontology can at best render possible the phenomenological datum; it cannot serve to discredit or nullify data by declaring on *a priori* grounds what data are possible, or in general what is and what is not possible within the whole of being. My argument, it should be repeated, is not directed against ontology; it is directed only against those ontologies that have forgotten memory.

8

Ontological Conditions
of Value

SINCE ONTOLOGY wants to know how things are possible, and since somehow there are values, ontology must have something to say about them too. Not much, since what ontology can contribute here is fairly meager and rather obvious, but sometimes the most obvious is the most easily forgotten. Let us begin by imagining something ontologically complete; that is, for its being it requires no other thing. It is, in short, an "absolute." Let us further endow such an absolute with consciousness. Since such a consciousness is the consciousness of an absolute, it must be exclusively "self-consciousness," since any consciousness of something other than itself would destroy the very completeness we have attributed to it. Our absolute being would then be pure reflexivity. Would such a being experience its own being as "valuable"? If this hypothetical entity seems preposterous at the outset, we might recall that it is an entity of just this sort that has haunted philosophy almost from its inception; it is the formal description of Parmenides' Being Itself, of Aristotle's God, of Spinoza's Blessedness of Mind, of Hegel's Absolute as Spirit. It is the transcendental ego of this book. And where do good and evil lie for such an entity? They have in their polar opposition disappeared in an ineffable "blessedness," in a value "beyond good and evil." This is "nirvana," sometimes called "nothingness."

These considerations may appear somewhat remote from any discussion of good and evil or values and disvalues pertinent to human existence. For if anything is obvious, it is that human existence, and all other existents as well, are incomplete, and therefore "needy" of something not themselves in order to be themselves. No existent can be ontologically complete, since the moment it became so it would pass from existence into eternity, a heterogeneous mode of being. To exist is to relate in some way to other existents. An existent that did not inherently require other existents would automatically constitute a universe of being, timeless, to which nothing could happen not already implicated by its own nature, and which in effect would be synonymous with Parmenides' One. The One does not exist or become; it simply is. These propositions themselves are not empirical generalizations, but simply logical consequences of meanings.

And so if anything is to exist, it requires other existents besides itself; this requirement is rooted in the essence of finite existences, and is not something added to that essence by consciousness. If such an ontologically needy existent were conscious, its consciousness of what it required would be its desire. And what desire desires is precisely that which the existent needs in order to exist. And since the existence in question is not merely bare existence, but existence of a certain sort, or in a certain style, its desires or conscious needs will be modulated accordingly. A man who only wanted to "exist" would be at the bottom of life.

Whatever is desired, whether it is a thing, an action, a person, or whatever, is valued; to the needy existent, the thing it desires is needed to complete itself. The "value" of that other thing, then, is nothing else than its capacity to fulfill the needs of the existent needing it; and that particular capacity is itself of an ontological or factual order. The thing desired either can or cannot fulfill the intentions of the desire directed to it. The intentions of the desire, of course, are always to unite the needy being with the needed one; that union or completion is the value hoped for in the desired thing. And so while every desire is a form of pain, what it desires is its own extinction as desire in the pleasure of complete being. All values, then, are translatable into pleasures, joys, or satisfactions, the consciousness of an existent possessing for a moment and in a certain respect the blessedness of eternal being. But it hardly needs saying that no existent human being needs only one thing; and so even our moments of pleasure are shadowed by uneasiness or concern for all the other things we need but do not have.

For a thing to have value—or to be the "bearer" of value, as Scheler puts it—is for it to be a means of completion for the entity requiring it; the completion itself is the value. As some form of completion, each value is a quasi absolute; it is one mode in which the needy existent is no longer needy, but simply is. In that respect it is "satisfied." The thing valued bears its value only in relation to the existent needing it; if nothing needed anything else, nothing else could bear any value for it. And so everything in the world acquires value only insofar as it is necessary for some other thing, with its own specific nature and constitution. The value each thing has is its ability to complete the needy thing. Value does not inhere in a thing, but in what the thing promises: the joy or satisfaction of a quasi-complete being. The value that anything bears is therefore relative to other existent things; and yet what anything of value bears is the promise of something itself absolute, value. Values are therefore absolutes, borne by things in their relations to other existents that need them. An experienced value is the experience of a mode or moment of complete or absolute being.

This is in accord with Plato, for whom the Good, Being, and the One are identical.

Some Applications

Supposing some such thing to be the case, of what possible use is it? Precious little, if someone should suppose that either this or any general theory of value would enable him to reach any conclusions whatever about human existence. And yet this may be the utility of such considerations after all: the prevention of any supposed descent from ontology or any general theory of value into the existent human scene. After a little further examination, perhaps it will be more than sufficiently evident that at least on our own assumptions about value, there can be no universal principles that can "decide" questions of value; that the human scene remains as free and open as we find it; and that decision is precisely as creative as many existentialists would have it. Our ontology of value would then serve the negative purpose of rendering impossible any dogmatic morality without thereby removing the grounds for action.

Our general ontological theory of value can trace the origin of value only in the domain of being called "existence." And so it would be no more valid for one existent than for another. Even the "consciousness" it postulated was nothing more than a sentience, a feeling or desire. But a human being is not simply the sentience of a body. If the needs of an existent were mentioned, the existent was not further specified. A human consciousness, on the other hand, is not merely the consciousness of physical wants. It is at the same time reflexive; that is, it is also conscious of itself as consciousness. In a word, it is a *self*. The human existent, then, is an existent self that distinguishes itself from its body and has its own needs apart from the needs of its body. It is now from the standpoint of this existent that we must look at value, at good and evil. Values now must be values for the self.

Since values can be borne only by those existents that my existence requires for its existence, the very prizing of existence puts me beyond the sphere where anything can be either good or evil. The choice of or consent to existence is the *a priori* condition for the arising of values phenomenologically. This is only another way of saying that good and evil are goods and evils for *life,* inherently life-bound, and senseless without that presupposed choice. This may seem to be contradicted by philosophy's long tradition of proposing "eternal goods," the love or the knowledge of eternal things, as opposed to existent things in their transiency and ambiguity. For Plato, the soul "recovered" its real self by treating existents as occasions for its reminiscence of the eternal forms it "knew" at one time, but "forgot" through the misfortune and confusion of birth. For Spinoza, blessedness was the intuitive knowledge of the place of mind in nature, or seeing all things *sub specie aeternitatis.* This was the only good that was stable, independent of the vicissitudes of modal existence, pure act devoid of suffering, a joy as opposed to a pleasure. For Schopenhauer, we escape from both the illusions of individuation and the swings of pleasure and pain by the will-less contemplation of Platonic forms in the arts, and by the suppression of the will to live altogether, in a radical asceticism. From this point of view, is not positive value located beyond existence, in the domain of the ideal, the eternal, the transcendental?

Yet the opposition may be only specious and verbal. For, first of all, if "eternal goods" achieve their value simply as reliefs from the inherent pains of the domain of existence, then they remain bound to that troubling existence as an escape from it, so that without any reference to existence they would not be goods at all, but indifferent entities or states of mind. But with the possible exception of Schopenhauer, it seems doubtful that any philosopher in this tradition intended any such thing. Next, if this eternal blessedness were indeed a re-cuperation of the soul's own transcendental nature, then those eternal-ideal entities must be envisaged as essentially bound up with the transcendental soul, "seen before birth," or perhaps as "innate ideas" or as its essential functioning character. In this case, the transcendental ego already "has" its own blessed-ness, cannot not have it, since it is nothing but an eternal im-plicate of it; existence itself can only appear as the worst disaster the self ever experienced, and the only sensible solution is to get out of existence as soon as possible. It is doubtful whether this interpretation is anything more than a caricature of the tradition in question. Perhaps, then, the opposition be-tween the transcendental ego and the existing ego has been conceived too abstractly?

For us life is not a transcendental good, since that represents a contradiction in terms; there can then be no transcendental duty to live and conversely none not to live. Prior to the radi-cally unjustifiable choice of existence, there is neither good and evil nor duty. Once this choice has been made, things that favor the type of existence continually chosen by the particular transcendental ego are designated as good, and things that hinder it are designated as evil. Good and evil then revert to the free choice of the transcendental ego, which can do no other than make "free choices," and since that ego can permit nothing beyond it, its choice is entirely and completely "justified" by each ego for itself. This "choice" in which good and evil are grounded is itself a transcendental choice—that is, is timeless—and constitutes the basis for what Kant and Schopenhauer called one's "intelligible character," not far from the "existential project" of Sartre. It is, of course, never a matter put up for deliberation at some particular date in the self's autobiography. It may be revoked at any time, but only after it is made.

To choose existence is for us to choose first of all to animate our bodies. And so existence is immediately specified through the given body. The human body then at once specifies that transcendental choice into a bodily existence, and becomes an "instinct" to live; and progressively not an instinct merely to live, but to live in a certain way. And so what began as a transcendental act, while remaining transcendental, at the same time is specified into the particular concrete life of each human being. But all the way along, each specification offers further opportunities for choice. One is born with a certain sex, certain faculties, certain physical tendencies. But these may be either affirmed or denied, or both affirmed and denied, or modified in innumerable ways. One's sex can be affirmed or denied; one's odd shape may be ignored, overcompensated for, a matter of pride, shame, or indifference. And so on through the whole tale of one's family, social situation, friends, country, age, and so on. And in the end, one can retrospectively regret the whole affair; the Greek anthology contains the remarkable judgment: "Better never to be born, second best to die young." Or conversely one can rejoice in it; Kant is supposed to have said: *Alles ist gut.* Perhaps each life, if it has the opportunity at the end, is best understood as some nuance of retrospective judgment upon itself; existence becomes autophenomenal and autobiographical.

Within this most general horizon, we must discriminate two conspicuous subtypes of value, the "moral" and the "social." Another chapter discusses the moral from a point of view akin to this. If the moral is inherently or by definition a matter of principle, universality, or generally valid law, it is immoral if it takes those claims to be ultimate, since the moral, so defined, is nothing but a subtype of value, and what may be valid for it need not be valid for the larger category of value. There is therefore a possibility that the moral, in its specificity and narrowness, may conflict with the freer and more universal "value." Or, to put the matter more positively, there may be values more ultimate and final than moral ones; the chapter on the transcendent in love suggests this very possibility. In other contexts, the relevant value may well be the moral.

And so with the social. The realm of justice, equality, consideration—the whole domain outlined by the concluding section of Hegel's *Philosophy of Right*—indeed does define a very substantial value. We are under no absolute obligation to value it, contrary to Hegel's opinion; but we oppose or ignore it at a very considerable cost, a cost we may or may not wish to pay. The transcendental freedom of choice, then, as we have already seen, is not a recommendation to anarchy, license, "conservatism," or, in effect, a recommendation of any value whatever. It is designed only to put values in their ontological place, and to remove the spuriously absolute or rational character that has been attributed to certain forms of value by those who try to ground it on something other than a transcendentally free choice.

It would be a mistake to divorce the general consideration of value from ontology, by isolating it in some "value theory." Values for me represent the way I finally want to be, and therefore the way I want you, my society, and everything else to be. Value, then, of its own nature implies what I choose to be and what I decide ought to be. Some things are as I would have them; others are not. Value is in both places, and not forever in an abstract "ought." In any event, the most general value, or the most universal ought-to-be, is, conversely, *being* as a value, or as it ought to be. The transcendental choice to exist at all, with its progressive development and specification, reflects itself in each human project. The project, continually realizing itself and continually stretching toward a future of life, itself defines its own relevant world of existence. Our values serve to define for us what is "real" in existence; in other words, they disclose a world. What is to appear and count as a world for each man will ultimately be defined by his ultimate values. One's experiential circumscribing of a world, seemingly a "factual" matter, is rather a function of his choice of values, reverting ultimately to that transcendental choice to live at all, to "allow" existence in general to reveal itself to the ego. Implied in that transcendental choice is the prizing of what existence shows. If that is prized, we therefore try to preserve it, as a prize fetched from the original fall into existence. And how can it be preserved in its own existential character, as opposed to the ideal "truths" it illustrates, except through memory? Memory, then, is one essential way in which the transcendental ego preserves itself amid the distraction and chaos of its chosen existence. It therefore is an essential factor in ontological autobiography. The project or projects that constitute any given life form another; it is these projects that disclose the shape of existence, a world, to the ego.

9

The Immorality of Morality

THE MUSEUM OF MAN in Paris exhibits a mask from the New Hebrides, chalk-white, with thin wispy hair on a large domed head, a head that almost seems to have sucked up within it the entire life of the body. The lips are thin and tight, the cheeks are sunken, and two hard and terrified eyes stare out from black rings and hollows. Nothing is known of its original model, but it is not hard to guess what he was: a missionary, come to teach the Melanesians a better life, to bring the joyous gospel of salvation. What we see is the spirit of Moses' "Thou shalt not" and of Jesus' "Thou shalt"—each a command to be disobeyed at dreadful peril. In a word, we see the spirit of *morality*.

Now this might seem questionable or offensive. Morality carried to the point of white-faced opposition to life, some might say, is no longer morality at all, but rather puritanism, from which we have now happily freed ourselves. It is puritanism and not morality, it might be urged, that carries moral law to the point of paroxysm, turning what initially had some justification into something that finally has none. It is only puritanism that moves from a purification of life to purification *from* life, and is focused so narrowly on an abstract ideal that its face resembles the skull the Melanesian artist saw. Today we suppose ourselves to have made much progress in this department; no one any longer takes morality that seriously. We are more relaxed about the whole matter; our criteria are more humane; we make room for exceptions; we understand human weakness; we don't push anything too far. My equivalence of the spirit of morality with death was therefore an exaggeration or an outmoded idea. Today we imagine ourselves both moral and friendly to life.

Now, whatever is to be said of our practice, it should be said that the theory of our new moral friendliness to life is little short of ludicrous. For, as a new principle, it must say that the moral good becomes even better through a tolerant admixture of what our morality itself must regard as immoral—that is, that the commandment to pursue the best must be relaxed at times; the best becomes even better or more delicious when flavored with a pinch of the worst. Thus we can remain men of moral principle but escape the perils of any fanaticism of principle by adding some parentheses about "difficulties of applying principles," "singular circumstances," and the "finitude of knowledge." At the same time that we announce a conception of the good, whether we dress it in religious or in philosophical clothes, we wink to show we too are human; that is, we do not take what we say too seriously. Now the wink speaks well for our common sense, but it is disastrous for our theory. And so here I should like to present reasons for believing (1) that every morality, whether religiously expressed as commandments of God or philosophically expressed as reason applied to the conduct of life, depends upon principle; (2) that, in the question to which all moralities address themselves, no exception can be admitted; (3) that no universal principle offered by any morality can have any bearing at all on life; (4) that all moralities turn themselves immediately into their opposite, the immoral (hence the paradoxical title of this chapter); and (5) that, if the whole religious and philosophical theory of moral principle is disastrous, we must find another way of illuminating this most decisive area of our concerns, a way that we may hope will not simply introduce one more principle.

It must be granted that men passionately pursued and shunned and fought things long before philosophers endeavored to sum it all up in a conception of an ideal of life, a standard, a principle, a universal, which would grasp the very essence of value. And I think it must also be granted that in fact this is exactly what men do today after some thousands of years of philosophical clarification and religious revelation. Men have not engaged in bitter disputes over the question of whether or not they should make choices, since none of us can avoid choosing, but over the principles in accordance with which their choices are made—their "guiding principles."

The secret aim of all such principles is to create a certain type of man, the moral man—or, as we say, the "man of principle." If you are not a man of principle, you are, of course, unprincipled, or immoral. No one knows what you will do next; you are unreliable, you cannot be trusted, and, in effect, you are on the verge of exclusion from the human community, which is composed of those who "recognize principle," some common moral law. The secret ambition of morality is not merely to clarify any particular life, but to form each life in such a way that ideally all of us must become "men of principle." The principle in question can be grasped intellectually as a *concept;* it is a universal ideal. It is "universal" in the sense that it applies to all men, under all circumstances, and with absolute validity. It formulates once and for all what an ideal man must be; it supplies standards for judgment and standards for self-criticism. We should feel shame when we compare what we have done and are with what the principle declares we ought to be. This attempt to grasp intellectually, by means of a principle, the universal concept of man, both to confirm judgments about men and to supply an ideal to which they are obliged to aspire, is the essence of the ethical and religious understanding of human life. If philosophy hopes to understand or even prove that principle, religion will take it on faith. No matter, both aim at principle. And yet there are serious reasons for doubting the project's validity, whether it is undertaken by the philosopher or the true believer. The transcendental singularity and freedom of each man is incompatible with any principle whatever.

If duty or the good is located in a principle, no matter what that principle is, then obviously no exception can be admitted. No matter how duty or the good is understood, the project of defining it either fails, in which case our point is granted, or succeeds, in which case any exception can appear only as evil or an unjustifiable lapse. This is not puritanism, but simply the dialectic of principles. No ideal could tolerate holidays from what it envisages. And so the Lord of Israel could never have commanded, "Thou shalt not kill, except occasionally," or "Thou shalt have no other gods before me, usually." Nor can Kant's categorical imperative issue its commandment to act solely from motives of duty, only to add in a whisper that self-interest is acceptable too from time to time, as a relief. Even the smiling "greatest happiness principle" eventually must frown on those who do not pursue their own and others' happiness, even if only occasionally. If such ideals, or any others presented as principles, admit exceptions, then they confess their own

incompetence. They are not principles, but only passing remarks, to be qualified as each understands them.

One might raise the question why men ever sought to understand their lives by means of principles in the first place, so
that eventually they even desired to live according to what they
had conceived, and finally to turn themselves into principles.
But this would carry us too far afield. It may be sufficient to
remark that this project is itself a special free option, in no
way binding upon the transcendental freedom of the subject.
But it does tend to hollow the eyes and thin the hair, as the
Melanesian artist saw.

To whom are such values valuable? That is, to whom is the
good good, and to whom is duty a duty? As a principle, the
good or duty—that is, value—can present itself to our minds
only as a universal abstraction whose proper correlate is equally
an abstraction: man, rational will, or some surrogate—deity,
nature, or history. The more formally values are conceived, the
more formally that entity for whom they are eventually to be
values must be conceived. Duty itself, as the formal principle
of each moral volition, can have as its correlate only the *form*
of the will, and not that will in its concrete existential exercise.
Its exercise may have a form—indeed, must have some form,
since everything is susceptible to formalization—but if formalization is simply that act of mind by which the principle or
universal of something is noticed, what must be observed is
that it is by the same token an act of *omission;* and what is
omitted is the existential uniqueness and contingency, the par-
ticularity of that very volition being formalized. Finally, it is
only within the domain of existence itself that the choice of
value, and therewith its very value, has any sense at all. Logical
and eternal correlates between the essence of value and the
essence of him to whom the value must be valuable may be
abstracted; and yet the domain from which they are abstracted

is the very domain in which they retain whatever sense they might have. In short, mankind, rational will, the personal or social essence can actually choose nothing, and therefore they can achieve no actual values; they are nothing but essences. They may be illustrated, but as essences they must profoundly falsify what illustrates them. What the abstraction abstracts from is the essential here.

When moral principles that admit of no exceptions are given out, they demand of the person to whom they are addressed nothing less than that he himself become a principle—that is, that abstraction to which such principles must logically address themselves. And this is the essence of the incoherence as well as the immorality of every morality.

Behind such an effort to grasp the human good or human duty, it is not difficult to perceive the motive to understand once and for all what I should do and be, what every man should do and be, and in effect to abridge the enigmas and mysteries of human individuality and history with a concept. When one reflects upon the work such a concept is called upon to perform—to grasp here and now those values and aspirations that animate the existing transcendences that we are—the project seems as preposterous as it is pernicious. The trouble with these reflections is not that they do not help us to know what value is, but that there is nothing here to know. The question lies entirely in the domain of existential choice and not in that of timeless knowledge. If some speak of values as "right" and "wrong," they should understand that what they are doing is simply affirming some values and rejecting others; there can be no question of values being logically "correct" or "incorrect," "right" or "wrong."

Nor can the question be resolved by introducing such subjectivities, spurious or not, as God, nature, or history. For some, absolute value is what God wills as disclosed by either reason or faith. If reason is understood as a purely cognitive power, which sees or grasps what ought to be, we can only reply that what it sees may indeed be seen, but what it sees is a *choice,* which returns us to where we were at the outset. If reason is understood as "practical reason," it is but another name for a formalization of the will. If the whole matter is frankly stated as faith, we have no quarrel with it; the faith in question is identical with what we have called choice. In either case, "God" has the function of expressing simply the finality with which any ultimate choice understands itself. The same applies to notions that the good can be understood as the aim of nature or history. The question whether nature and history have aims we can ignore; if they do, then we revert to our own choice of either affirming or denying those aims; if they have no aim, then it is again up to us to choose the way in which we wish to direct them.

If the value is a value only for God, nature, or history, but not for any existing man, then God, nature, or history may indeed enjoy its benefits, but can there be any necessity for men to agree? And since it is always existing men who must suffer and do the work of realizing these superpersonal values, helping God, nature, or history to triumph, it is hard to see precisely what, short of self-loathing, could be men's motives. And yet no doubt every motive finds its own place in the human breast.

Perhaps we may consult numbers to resolve what must remain an individual choice: the greatest happiness of the greatest number of persons. And unquestionably, values for a society do indeed seem to have greater weight than those realized by a single individual. From Plato and Aristotle through Hegel, Mill, and Marx, the theme has been argued at sufficient length. But the style of social and political values of each person must redound to choice and not to conclusions drawn from a sup-

posedly objective consideration of the values themselves. If a
man chooses the most antisocial behavior possible, he is neither
more correct nor more incorrect than the greatest social benefactor; in addition, we social beings have every right to behave
in any way we consider appropriate toward the man whose
behavior we judge to be antisocial, and not to envy his choice.

Values in principle cannot be considered objectively without
by that very act ceasing to be values. An objective reason may
well trace out the probable consequences of choices; but it
cannot choose or in its strict purity even have the faintest idea
of what a value is. Value is a course of action as it appears to
choice in the light of reason; choice is the subjective act of
preference. Reason can prefer nothing. It cannot even prefer
itself. The choice to think or behave consistently is a choice—a
choice, moreover, for which no reason can be given. If I prefer
to act inconsistently, reason may be offended by the rejection
of her charms; but it cannot accuse that choice of being any
more irrational than an opposite choice would be. And, it
should hardly require adding, a choice remains subjective even
when many or all subjectivities agree on it.

So far, these considerations have themselves been excessively
abstract and fundamentally negative. Their burden has been to
make clear that morality is invariably a question of principle,
that principles permit no exceptions, purporting to be valid
for all acts and for everyone, and that, when they are so understood, their only correlative subject must necessarily be not any
existing man, but the form of all men—another abstraction,
which no man is or could be except by self-delusion, and which
could never make a single choice.

If all this seems too trite to mention, I submit that in fact it
is almost too much to bear. It is not easy to give up all guide-
lines, all moralities, finally all intelligibility of human life, all
supposition that there is something that can be known, in the

interest of being, with Nietzsche, "faithful to the earth." If we give up every aspiration to "know" our lives, to acquire through the years, through experience, and through sharpness of thought some mastery of the whole affair, what indeed is left? Have we not abandoned thought itself, reason with its principles, and finally human society?

At first glance, yes; perhaps at second glance, no. But before we go on to investigate that topic, perhaps it might be helpful to recall that every morality of principle, every standard that has been set up to indicate what each singular person should do, has at this point turned into its opposite. While such ideals wish to indicate the goal of life, they indicate a goal only for someone not ourselves—for God, for human nature, for who knows what?—and hence become a form of immorality. And then there are ourselves; when all is said and done, it is each man who has to decide if anything is to have sense to him. The effort to think out a morality for everyone (and all moralities must be for everyone) founders on the sober fact that in the last analysis everyone is an individual; everyone is and always has been only himself, which is quite enough.

So far, I have spoken negatively: no principles of human life, no absolute person to whom it may all make sense, even if it makes none to us; in short, no philosophical and religious theory of value that is tenable to any existent man unless he wills it to be so, which isn't exactly the point of such views. If to abandon reason here seems like pure folly, I should like to suggest finally some virtues in abandoning philosophical reason and religious beliefs about human life. In effect, these virtues all add up to the same thing: to our restoration in thought to what we were originally, are now, and must remain —transcendences in existence.

And so let us look at the secret aspirations of religious and philosophical ethics so that we may be quite certain about what has gone wrong; and then let us see if there is not another way of looking at all these matters, a way that it is to be hoped can be "faithful to the earth" without secretly imposing yet another moral principle in disguise.

Species other than man run more or less according to type, so that a lion does not have to decide how a lion should act, when to roar and when not; but man is most himself when he exercises the freedom that both enables and requires him to choose what is to be essential in his life. In short, as the existentialists never tire of insisting, men must decide their own essence, choose it. It is not biologically given; or, insofar as it is biologically given, it constitutes only the background or situation for what must be decided. What each man is to decide is simply what he is to be; that is inherently a matter of decision or it cannot even pretend to be a value. If it is a decision that each must make, it cannot be deduced from pure reason, it cannot be generalized from empirical research, and it cannot descend from revelation. All of these so-called "essences" of what it is to be human represent nothing but various possibilities; they cannot in themselves have any authority whatsoever. Authority can be conferred on them only by each man's own consent.

In short, man is not a fixed essence; there is no human nature. The only nature we can be said to have resides in the freedom to decide what is essential, a freedom that stones, stars, plants, and animals do not have in any noticeable degree, and which we attribute to ourselves as our "nature," the nature of what has no nature.

If any such thing is roughly the case, there can be no philosophical theory of the moral and no religious revelation of it either. Both philosophy and religion, in this sense, wish to short-circuit the very source of value: each man's own free decision. And in the long run, both would, if successful, render our decisions worthless. If I can already know what the ideal man is, then I do not have to decide it; it represents a given, and my decision is confined to the relatively trivial matter of whether I will live up to that preformulated ideal or not. But the only genuine question concerns that ideal itself; it is that which I and I alone must decide. And it is a *decision,* and not a revelation or the conclusion of an argument. So while there can be a history of collective and individual ideals, styles of life, options, there can be no knowledge of their value in advance

If this sounds depressing for the pretensions of philosophy and religion, it is in fact healthy for existence. What could be worse than a situation in which we, here and now, could know what man really is, the correct ideal image, and read history and ourselves as simply approaching or receding from that known ideal? This would instantly render both human history and our own lives profoundly meaningless. We would be nothing but more or less smudged blackboard illustrations of a supposedly known essence, "human nature." And yet what is our individual task but to create in our own historical way those very ideals? Both religion and philosophy, so understood, would be successful only at the price of extinguishing the very sense of our living existence.

But beyond this, we have to consider those values in our lives that conspicuously do not and cannot fall under any principle—all those values that are conferred upon events spontaneously, without reference to any principle at all. Fun is one value frequently overlooked by philosophical and religious minds. A life without it would hardly be endurable, and yet it can never be generated by the will, in accordance with some principle; nor can there be a revelation as to what must be fun. Charm is another; there are "charm schools" that claim to teach the principles of charm, and we have all seen their highly uncharming products exercising their techniques upon us. Is charity to be commanded from above as a duty? But to give because one must is to drain the gift of its inherent meaning. If giving is a duty, the recipient then has a corresponding right to the gift. But then in what sense is it still a gift? Shall we love according to principle? Or as a duty? Or because it is already inscribed in the essence of man? But what lover would want that? Unless love proceeds from the very spontaneity of each existing man, it is no longer love, but rather a necessity having no freely conferred value, or an obligation proceeding from who knows where. And the arts! Are there principles of art? There have been generalizations from what has been deemed art so far; but to imagine for an instant that these generalizations from the past have authority over the future would be to install the worst academicism in the very heart of what must be fresh if it is to exist at all. Can there be principles of freshness?

In short, the very aspiration of philosophy and religion to sum up once and for all what is best, what is holy, what is beautiful founders on the simple fact that there is a germ of freedom in man, which, after all, is the only dignity we have and the only thing that distinguishes us from the rest of being. How ludicrous to dream of deciding here and now what everyone *must* do, of establishing standards for all men, past, present, and future! Upon analysis the dream turns into a nightmare and finally extinguishes that very freedom which was the condition of being human, of human dignity, of creation. Every morality, as we have seen, is a morality of principle; and since every principle must necessarily end in condemning what is not a matter of principle, every morality must therefore turn into its dialectical opposite, immorality; and what we are left with finally is something that resists every effort to comprehend, to understand, to grasp theoretically— that is, transcendentally free human beings who must create their lives and not have them predetermined in the form of an ideal before they have even lived.

10

Some Phenomenological
Notes on Horror

WEBSTER'S definition of the word "horror" relates it to a series of other terms, "fear," "fright," "alarm," "panic," "dread," "dismay," "consternation," and "terror." It is said to be a "painful" emotion, a "repugnance" or "aversion" accompanied by "bristling" and "shuddering." Let us suppose that we know how to use the term; does this mean that we are now fully equipped to analyze the thing itself? Having related it to enough traits to identify it, have we thereby exhausted its structure? Or is there something more to be seen in this particular emotion?

First of all, here we are interested only in the internal sense or structure of the feeling, nothing else. We therefore at once set aside questions about its physiological or unconscious factors. We do not deny that such factors are present; we simply exclude them from consideration to whatever extent they remain purely physiological or purely unconscious. If they appear within the feeling and to the feeling, they should appear in our description, but they have then ceased to be purely physiological or purely unconscious. So far as we feel horror, phenomenologically it is much as if we were in a theater. To judge the play it is entirely unnecessary to know how the stage is held up or who pulls the curtain. There is a phenomenon, and it is with this phenomenon that we shall be concerned. Further, phenomenological descriptions of consciousness take priority over any inquiry that looks for causes or grounds or consequences of consciousness; for any such inquiry must find grounds for consciousness itself, and if consciousness has not received its appropriate description in phenomenological terms, how shall we ever judge whether we have found its adequate grounds? The cause must be adequate to the effect; hence if consciousness should be an effect, we must know very exactly what that effect is. With this in mind, we now omit all mention of the thalamus, the endocrine glands, musculature, electrical conductivity of skin, and sweat. If horror essentially involves "bristling" and "shuddering," then the man who feels horror will also feel himself bristling and shuddering, and will not have to make inferences from them or ask another. In passing, it might not be inappropriate to remark that only he with bristles can bristle, and not everyone who feels horror has the required bristles. As for shuddering, yes and no; unquestionably we do shudder at some kinds of horror, but not all. Some discriminations are needed.

But before going further, let us look at some examples. Obviously, horror is felt for the horrible; and while this particular correlation is hardly very illuminating, it will serve as a guiding thread. The horrible in all its varieties will serve as a clue to both the feeling of horror itself and to him who feels horror. Horror is the horrified apprehension of what is to that feeling a horrible object; horror, then, apprehends the horrible, and the horrible is apprehended or felt only by horror. We know that anything is horrible only because we feel horror for it. For what, then, do we feel horror?

Perhaps the commonest examples of the horrible are physical: bodily defects or injuries. Burned faces, the empty eye sockets of old Oedipus, slaughterhouses, sideshow freaks, the monstrously fat woman, the man without arms, the child with flippers for limbs, the accident on the street . . . these can supply us with a horror verging on nausea or disgust. Here the very body recoils from what it sees; as Webster says, there is a shuddering. But the horrible is surely not restricted to the injured, defective, or monstrous body. There is also the horror of the psychopathic ward, the mentally ruined, the violent and the vacant. With both of these types of the horrible, the physical and the psychological, it is as if the most basic vital aspirations were offended. But there are horrors of other kinds, horrors that offend the very spirit. Mr. Kurtz in *The Heart of Darkness* judges himself and the whole of Europe with the phrase "The horror of it all!" Ivan Karamazov has his "dossier against God," in which he has collected incidents that are radically incompatible with any moral governance of the world. Defects of character, malicious action, and a final meaninglessness of life are horrors to the spirit, which, like the body, has its own life and affirmations, and therefore can be shocked. At this end of the scale we find the horrors against which religion and philosophy recoil and look for "answers." The religious man feels a sneaking suspicion that there may be no God, or, if there is, that he himself is excluded from God's presence. Pascal describes his horror of the endlessness of space and time. And it is not difficult to detect something amounting to horror in those rational philosophers who devote their very lives to the demonstration that reality is not merely knowable, but known to themselves, and that what they know is not some ghastly illusion, not their own arbitrary language or fictions of their own production. Why otherwise the energy devoted to demonstrations of the validity of reason? To be sure, this particular sort of horror primarily afflicts rationalists, who demand absolute intelligibility; the empiricists, with an easier temperament, settle into unintelligibility at the outset, and, making no such demands, are not offended when they are not met. Or perhaps they would bristle and shudder if there *were* some vast intelligibility to things which had escaped them.

Children love the horrible, and we give them an entire evening every year to indulge themselves in it. Come Halloween, what do they do but make themselves into ghosts, skeletons, witches, monsters of every sort? Primitive people frankly love the horrible, and rightly find a close connection between it and the beautiful; young men must have their scars, and tribal masks are never idealizations of the human, but transformations of the human face into that of a bird, crocodile, snake, or insect. The taste of the eighteenth century found these simply ugly; now we tend to find them interesting compositions. In truth they are probably neither, but rather expressions of a certain wisdom of the sensibility that demands a hint of the horrible in every particular beauty. Baudelaire was the poet of this particular ambiguity, the flowers of evil; his favorite painter was Delacroix, who painted Moroccan lions tearing one another to pieces, frightful battles of men against men and of men against animals, and finally harem scenes of such mindless voluptuousness as faintly to sicken us with a new kind of horror.

The communal sense of the horrible is fixed in cultural images. The ancient Greeks, who appear to some as sunny athletes of nature, were of course virtually transfixed by the horrible. There were Oedipus killing his father and marrying his mother, Medea murdering her children, and Thyestes making a meal of his. The mythological landscape was populated with monsters—the Sphynx, the Minotaur, the Cyclopes—half human, half bestial, epitomized in Medusa, with her hair of snakes and her petrifying gaze. Long before that the Lord had rained fire and brimstone on Sodom and Gomorrah, killed the first-born son of every family in Egypt, and required the Israelites to bring their best animals to the tabernacle, there to be flayed and butchered, their blood sprinkled "round about upon the altar," and their severed parts burned, because "an offering made by fire" was "of a sweet savour unto the Lord." Little wonder, then, that the Israelites later followed the example of the Canaanites and piously burned their children. The Christian world, with its gospel of salvation, was also not unacquainted with the horrible. Its God was nailed hand and foot to an upright pole with a crossbeam attached at the top, and all the early saints were martyrs: St. Stephen, stoned to death; St. Sebastian, pierced with arrows till he resembled a human pincushion; St. Bartholomew, flayed and piously pictured with skin in hand. In literature the horrible was vividly elaborated by Dante, and in our own time we have almost an embarrassment of examples, from T. S. Eliot's hollow men through Kafka's violent tattooing machines and labyrinthine futilities right up to this morning's newspaper.

Now I have no intention of drawing any conclusions from these specific examples. If someone objects that he feels no horror whatsoever when Oedipus gouges out his eyes, I shall not argue that he ought to. Unquestionably, the occasions when men feel horror are widely variable; they vary from man to man, and for any particular man they vary according to time and circumstance, and according to the interpretation his sensibility places upon the given object. Hence at this point we need not consult any conclusions that have been reached by psychology, sociology, history, anthropology, or psychoanalysis.

These empirical findings could at best tell us the general class of objects that usually evoked horror in a given individual, epoch, or community. Since our own interest is in the structure of the feeling, it is a matter of indifference what the specific objects are. If a tribe in Africa feels no horror for a slaughter that makes our own flesh creep, then all we need to do is look elsewhere in the tribe to find what does make their flesh creep; their horror will have the same structure as ours, even though it may be directed to different objects.

Further, it is nothing to the point to object that the emotion of horror is *wrong*. If the fat lady of the circus should waddle into our own parlors, or if Oedipus should stagger in blind, we know at once what our reaction would be: as well-bred social creatures, we would stifle our horror in secondary reactions. In the presence of the fat lady there would be a deafening silence on the subject of monstrous corpulence, accompanied by reflections that she must be a glandular case and therefore "can't help it"; we would solicitously guide Oedipus to a chair, whether we thought he deserved it or not. But these reactions are secondary to a primordial sentiment, and in effect serve to protect us against the horror of the phenomenon. What is it that either can't be helped or was or was not deserved except the horrible itself? And so also for such cultivated sentiments as the comforting notion that if we understood the course of nature or the will of God, then nothing would seem horrible, but each thing would be comprehended as necessary, beautiful, or serving a higher end. All such reflections presuppose the primordial horror and seek either to justify it, to excuse it, or to eliminate it altogether; but what is it that is being justified or banished from the universe except precisely the horror that is our theme?

What are some features of the horrible? Webster notes one such feature: the horrible is profoundly *repellent*. And a glance at the range of the horrible discloses that there is also a range of levels at which we respond to it; it may be our most basic vital life that is repelled, our animal vitality and health, our ordinary consciousness, our basic sympathy for others, our spirit, or our reason. Every level on which we live and act is susceptible to the repellent offense of the horrible.

What repels in the horrible? Obviously, everything horrible is in some way deficient in what it should or might have. In short, concealed within the logic of the feeling itself is an ideal or a norm. When we encounter something that is markedly deficient according to its own norm, the deficiency grounds our·repulsion. Hence no one feels horror at a dog that lacks reason, but we may very well be shocked by a man who has lost his.

Yet the failure of any entity to realize the norm implicit in it is not in itself sufficient to account for horror. A broken-down Ford or Frigidaire hardly evokes horror, although a broken-down animal or man might very well do so. And so the beings from whose failures our own being recoils in horror must be alive; and not merely alive, but sentient. They must have desires and aims and be capable of feeling their own failures. Their failures must be such as to affect their lives, their powers of action, and ours through sympathy.

The next feature discernible in horror is not so frequently noticed: that while the horrible is profoundly repellent, it is also profoundly attractive. Augustine records in his *Confessions* that he found it hard to tear his eyes away from the gladiatorial contests; he both wanted to see and wanted not to see. The same is true of us; who but the fainthearted can resist a street accident? No sooner have the brakes screeched and the glass shattered than a crowd collects to feast its eyes. Books describing trench warfare, life in concentration camps, the medical experiments of Nazi doctors are always best-sellers, and a good deal of science fiction indulges the imagination with detailed descriptions of natural disorders and monstrosities. The horrible draws us to it, we feel we must see it, and we are held petrified by what we see. Horror is not, then, a simple revulsion. It is compounded of contrary movements, and it is precisely this contrariety of movement that holds the horrified one immobile.

Now it is absurd to declare such a feeling "morbid" when in the last analysis we find ourselves running to the accident anyway; and it is equally in bad faith to justify our primordial love for the horrible by excuses that we run to be of help, when most frequently we hinder it, or continue to stare even when there is no help to give. If politeness forces us to avert our gaze, we continue to stare out of the corners of our eyes. The horrible is irresistibly fascinating precisely because it appears evil to us.

Another feature of horror is that it is inevitably experienced as a shock. To grow accustomed to the horrible is to cease to experience it as horrible; hence nurses who live with the dying frequently feel no horror at what would turn a casual hospital visitor pale. A face without a nose is horrible enough, but if we met it suddenly as we turned the corner, it might be sickening. People who are subject to slow diseases find nothing horrible in their final state, whereas a friend who has not seen the decline is shocked.

One final feature: If a person has been made hideous by forces external to him, we may well view him with horror; but if he has deliberately inflicted hideousness upon himself, our horror is intensified. A hapless window washer who has slipped from a tenth-story ledge and now lies dead on the bloody sidewalk is almost certain to evoke our horror; but the corpse of a man who has jumped from that same ledge arouses even greater horror. Hence Sophocles had Oedipus put out his own eyes, in order to wring the last drop of horror from the situation. Accordingly, in order to diminish our own sentiment of horror, we endeavor to interpret it as the result of inevitable causes rather than of the will's own volition; for what good sense can we make of it when the free will turns against itself? Sophocles did this too: all the deeds that plunged Oedipus himself into horror had been ordained by the gods.

I believe that this circumstance arises from another: that the horrible presents us not merely with a finished state of diminished value in another, but with a possibility for our own action or suffering. Implicit in our fascination with the horrible is our recognition that the disaster might occur to us, that we might make the same decision.

Now let us gather together all these features into a general characterization of the horrible: horror, we shall say, is a shocked fascination with some disastrous choice or possibility of suffering that appears to us as radically evil.

What does such a feeling teach us about ourselves? Shock can disclose something about that which is shocked; for if anything is true, it is that reason in itself never is and never can be shocked by anything at all, let alone by what shocks us when we feel our flesh creep. All occasions and examples of the horrible are trite themes to our reflective intellect. Disease, death, corruption, insanity, and absurdity are very old stories indeed to reason, which can easily lump them all together under the heading "finitude." The horrible, then, does not stun our lucidity and reflectiveness, even though reflection may discover aspects of life that escape our immediate experience and present them for our horrified reaction. But even to discover these subtler aspects, it must be guided by an implicit sense of horror. In themselves reflection reflects and lucidity is clear; to see is not in itself to feel emotion. It is not our reason, then, that is stunned and fascinated by the horrible, but rather that dimension of ourselves which exists, lives, or acts. The name we select for this dimension is of less importance than its contrast with our reflective side. We can call it *élan vital* with Bergson, *Entwurf* with Heidegger, *projet* with Sartre, or more directly "life," provided this term is understood in the full range of its meaning, from a vital impetus or urgency through all the modulations of desire, volition, and aspiration of which a whole human being is capable. It is whatever acts in us that is stunned, and since there are many kinds of action, each with its corresponding suffering, there are many kinds of horror, each called forth by that which is appropriately horrible to it. Things really become horrible when action in its totality, or life altogether, or the dominant value of one's life, its "highest" aspiration, is threatened. For if only one occasion or possibility for action is denied, I may still have others. But when my life as a totality is threatened, then indeed the flesh creeps. Still, overarching the entire act of human existence is that level of lucidity or reflection which is not and cannot be shocked, except insofar as it is put into the service of life. Thus when we say that reason can be horrified by the possibility that everything is absurd, we are using shorthand to note a more complex situation: it is the *will* to reason, the *aspiration* to see everything as intelligible, that is stunned, not reason itself. Reason for its part finds rationality wherever it occurs, but has no particular desire in the matter. It is a living man with a wish to find everything intelligible who is horrified by the possibility that nothing may be intelligible. It is life that is horrified, not that nonvital lucidity which watches it all.

Why is life shocked by the horrible? But this is obvious; if our existences are acts, and if any act implicitly has a direction, an envisaged goal, which for that act is "value," obviously anything that threatens the very possibility of action—disease, death, insanity, disfigurement—offends the very aspiration of existence itself. To live is to exist optimistically. Life is a going concern, literally both going and concerned, and what keeps it going is its belief and concern in the attainability of its goals; it is already moving toward them. And so life must inherently be blind; to believe that one's goals are futile is to cut the nerve of one's will. The incurably blind optimism of existence has already prepared it for surprises and shocks. Life, we should say, is necessarily deceived: it cannot be concerned with all goals or with contrary goals, since it cannot move in every direction at once. To entertain conflicting beliefs or a tolerant sympathy for all possible values on this plane is to express nothing but existential confusion. Lucidity can pose every possible goal before it with equal comprehension; but it is not lucidity that acts. The act of human existence is necessarily directed, and therefore necessarily exclusive of alternatives; it is therefore necessarily deceived and necessarily subject to the shock of the horrible. It seeks life and runs upon death; it loves health but finds disease; it seeks happiness but finds insanity; it desires final meaning but finds the endlessness of time and space. To exist is therefore necessarily to be perpetually open to the sudden disillusionment of the antivital, or horrible.

But what should be said about the fascination of the horrible? Why do we not simply turn away from it, muster our forces to defeat it, or resign ourselves to its inevitability? Why do we secretly love to feast our eyes on what is intrinsically revolting? Freud said it was a "death wish," and no doubt it is, looked upon from the perspective of pure vitality. No doubt, if the horrible is everything we find ugly, evil, and antivital, and if we love to dwell on these things, it can only be because there is lodged within us a contrary principle that loves the opposite of life. But this is not the last word on the matter. Nor, for all their truth, do we find total satisfaction in the pragmatic analyses that find a certain utility in looking at what threatens our sense of life, in familiarizing ourselves with it, becoming accustomed to it, in order that we may escape its paralyzing effect. Children play with the masks of monsters so as to be better prepared to handle the monstrous when they encounter it unmasked. All this is no doubt true; but we do not remain children, yet we remain fascinated by the horrible. And there is no way of reconciling this naturalistic interpretation with the desire for death that Freud finds hidden in our souls. Since the pragmatic explanation depends on the desire for health and life alone, we must suspect it of wishing too strongly to see only this. For the obvious truth is that we do not always shun the evil in a single-minded impulse to live; we also plunge straight into it, deliberately embracing it, not for its educational value or because we innocently mistake it for something good, but precisely because we recognize it as evil. There is unquestionably, in my opinion, some truth to Freud's view that we can love the evil for the evil we find in it. This opinion is contrary to the views of Plato, Spinoza, and others, who find it irrational for man to seek what he "knows" to be evil to him. Such views put the whole burden of life upon failures of the intellect to know what is good. But other moralists argue, and to me rightly, that if there is a side to men that men themselves call evil, it manifests itself not so much in mistakes of their reason as in choices of their hearts. The fascination with the horrible is a *feeling,* and a very primitive one at that; and what the feeling feels is a diremption in itself: its feeling is a love-hate for what is felt as ugly and evil. Who on earth ever felt a fascination for the mistakes of his mind?

But if this is so, what can it teach us about ourselves, beings who can become fascinated by the possibilities of our own total and radical defeat? Here we find Freud of little help; his death wish was too pure a product of nineteenth-century naturalism, an "instinct," which expressed a natural tendency of complex, highly organized structures to collapse back into the simple. It was like a principle of fatigue; after the complex struggles of the daylight, we relapse back into sleep with a certain sigh of relief. And with such a metaphor, it all seems quite natural and therefore quite intelligible. But there are, I believe, profound difficulties in any view that finds final clarity of anything human in reversion to "instincts," "impulses," and the metabolism of protoplasm. For we do not wish to sleep in order to sleep forever, and how many of us would willingly fall asleep for an instant if we knew we could never wake up? And yet we are fascinated by death. Besides, there are types of the horrible that have little to do with any fatigue of the protoplasm. Is Pascal's horror of the endlessness of space and time to be understood as a phenomenon of protoplasm? But here we must object that we know far more of Pascal's sentiments than we do of the chemistry of protoplasm. My own conviction is that the phenomenon of horror, since it is directly a feeling and even at best only very remotely characterizable in biochemical terms, is best disentangled by further reflections on the feeling itself.

The horrified fascination with evil is, I have tried to argue, a love-hate for what is felt as good because it is apprehended as bad. The horrible thing has its seductive beauty, and our fascination with it is a compound of love and hate, and not a very rapid alternation between a pure love and an equally pure hate. For the sober fact is that the love is felt for the hateful; otherwise what we feel is not horror. Now this combination of opposites at one and the same time, both in our sentiment and in the object, is clearly impossible, says the "abstract understanding." Either love or hate, or a very rapid alternation, so rapid it escapes our notice; but not both at the same time in the same concrete act of emotion! The object is seen as either ugly or beautiful, or perhaps beautiful in one aspect and ugly in another. But in the phenomenon of horror the beautiful cannot be separated from the ugly; if we can isolate the two, we do not have the distinct phenomenon of horror, but only a hodge-podge of ideal constructs called love and hate. If love attracts and hate repels, as reason tells us, to combine both in a single feeling would be to combine attraction and repulsion, and the result could be neither the one nor the other; but when horror fixes us immobile in its stare, we find that in fact it is both. Our immobility in the face of horror does not result from the canceling out of both love and hate, as if two equal and opposite forces imposed themselves on a billiard ball. The horrible fascinates us not by reducing our souls to rest, but by arousing in us a most living feeling. What is it in us that can simultaneously live contrary passions?

Here I believe is the occasion to see in horror something more than the simple coming together of opposites: an aspect of consciousness that does not merely make a blend of opposites, but transcends them. Now when we recall the enormous range of kinds of things that we can experience as horrible, we see that the range is coextensive with all the things that can be considered the goods and evils of life. The goods demand no particular explanation; that we find them good is enough to justify our attraction to them. But what about the occasions when we find these same goods hateful and the most profound evils lovable? At what point can beauty be transformed into ugliness and ugliness into beauty, so that both are held together in solution? Such a transformation could occur only in response to a principle that is satisfied by neither pure goods nor pure evils, but can feel the good of evil and the evil of good. No such principle is thinkable on the plane of natural impulses. And again, while the particular name is not important, we may as well call it "freedom," fully recognizing that we have only clapped a name on a mystery. But if our freedom is indeed free, then it would be exactly that uncommitted and perpetually dissatisfied principle which could love everything it hates and hate everything it loves, choosing this or that but never anything with full heart. It therefore chooses life, but has one eye wistfully turned toward death; it loves justice, but can hardly conceal its secret love for injustice; it tries to act prudently, but can hardly wait for a holiday from the rational. But then it has no deep-seated affection for death, disease, and madness either; as soon as it comes close to them, it turns back to their opposites. In the end, we see in this absolute freedom a restless dissatisfaction with everything and an equal capacity to be seduced by anything. Such a principle is of course wild; it may learn to domesticate itself, but that is its own choice, and it can never do so without a lingering regret for its old open life. And I think we hardly need much argument to see in the perpetual and inherent ambiguity, restlessness, and dissatisfaction of our freedom a sign of something removed from the vital powers, impulses, and proclivities of protoplasm, nothing at all natural, but something that, though again the word is arguable, we can just as well term "absolute." It is that factor in life by which life itself is puzzled, a rather ambiguous friend of life values. From the perspective of life it is always dangerous, now friend, now foe, and therefore in its very absolute character something beyond life.

We can see in horror something of the character of that principle in us which is capable of this emotion: to hesitate between life and death, justice and injustice, the monstrous and the beautiful, is to express the radically ambiguous, ironic, and divided nature of men. Morbid, we say, in our insistence on our total devotion to the good, true, and beautiful. But if it is morbid, it also discloses its own beauties: the revelations that no finite good is wholly good, no finite beauty wholly beautiful, and no finite justice wholly just. Our ambiguity about all these, and finally about the very ideals themselves, is an expression of the inability of the absolute freedom in us to be absolutely satisfied by anything at all in life.

The horrified consciousness, then, transfixed by the beauty of everything ugly and the ugliness of everything beautiful, neither simply affirms nor denies life; it views both ironically, and in its irony can present us with a side of ourselves higher than life. The creature that can affirm nothing wholly or deny it either, while existentially confused if not paralyzed, is metaphysically sound; in the last analysis he expresses more vividly than anything natural the perpetual paradox between a transcendental ego and the existing ambiguities we are.

11

Some Notes on Death,
Existentially Considered

No sooner are we born than we know that we shall certainly die. Surely nothing is more commonplace than such "knowledge"; and yet the "way" in which we know that we shall certainly die is decisive, and decisive chiefly for the purposes of life. Let me then begin with a word on ways of knowing, or "philosophical methodology." Perhaps we can bring the problem into focus with an absurd question: Precisely how do we know that we shall certainly die? At first it might seem that we have learned it from experience; we know of people who have died, we have been told that everyone who has lived before us has died, and we can see no good reason why we ourselves should be exceptions. Besides, it is not only we that die; animals do too, and plants. Stones do not, but they were never alive in the first place. Further, no one has ever been known to live forever, with the possible exceptions of the Flying Dutchman and the Wandering Jew; but no one we know

has ever actually met either of them. And so it might seem
that if we do know that we must die, we know it on good
empirical grounds: our own observations of the evidence. I
have no wish to suggest that these observations are false, but I
do suggest that each man's knowledge of his own forthcoming
death has little or nothing to do with any such evidence. No
one has ever seriously tried to collect substantial statistical evidence on the question, and anyone who did would be regarded
as a fool. We already know that he would be wasting his time.
Besides, not all life is doomed to death; the lower forms of
one-celled plants and animals that reproduce by fission are
immortal, although it would be hard indeed to say precisely
which cell it is that lasts forever. As for the human scene, the
record must remain so incomplete as to be virtually worthless
for serious statistical study. And even if it could be rendered
complete or nearly so, in all strictness we should at most be
able to conclude that it is highly probable that we shall die.
But the point of all this is that we knew it with certitude be-
forehand; men always knew it; and therefore they knew it on
other grounds. And where could those other grounds be except
within us? That is, far from studying the evidence and concluding from it that we shall die, we know it from the very
structure of our own lives while still living. In short, the very
sense of life as it is lived implies the necessity of death. This
reflection on the sense of life as we live it from within, and
not as we observe it externally in others, is an informal way of
describing the method called phenomenology. Life is our
theme; and what are some of its structures as they disclose
themselves to us who live? With this shift of viewpoint we
bid good-bye to physics, biology, and sociology and attempt to
rejoin ourselves phenomenologically, as we must in any case,
as living beings living our lives.

Insofar as our own lives can become phenomena or appearances to ourselves, and insofar as the very life we live phenomenally bears the implication of death, we are faced with an odd problem: we clearly experience, in some sense, our own lives; but who ever experiences his own death?

My death is one thing that in principle I cannot experience or render "phenomenal." For as Epicurus said, while I am, Death is not; when Death is, I am not. And so no one has ever experienced his own death, which everyone is nevertheless convinced is absolutely certain, and which everyone dreads. We can perhaps feel for a moment the paradox of life dreading that which it will never experience, since death is the extinction of experiencing altogether. But there is no particular point now in pausing over this phenomenon, that the great enemy of life, death, can never be met head on. There are other, similar cases: my own existence is in some fashion always within the world, its very sense is to be within the world, and yet no one has ever seen anything like the world, and in principle never can. The world remains an unencounterable horizon within which everything we do see has its own sense; and yet the world itself is never encountered, never seen, and always eludes direct observation.

And so with death. Hence we must make do with what we have: life regarding death as its enemy but never being in a position to grapple with it directly or straightforwardly. The phenomenology of death is not a simple description of it, which would hardly be worth the trouble, since the description is completed in a word: nothing. It is instead an exploration of what death means to life, from the point of view of the living. Does it mean anything or nothing? Is it nothing but the great enemy who always wins?

Our responses to the certainty of death are most revealing of us; and perhaps in one way life is most properly considered as a response to death, its own extinction. What are some responses to death? Perhaps first of all there is a simple and flat opposition to it. To the extent that we are alive, we resist and oppose death, and that's that. To be alive is to affirm life and its values; death is the simple enemy of the whole project, to be opposed to the last. This plain opposition can never be forgotten. The absolute enmity between life and death cannot be softened or veiled by any other considerations. But then matters immediately become more complex: there is also most certainly within everyone something like a love of death— Freud's "death wish." In all of us, as we have observed, it expresses itself as a fascination with the horrible; in some it becomes a passion for suicide. For the profoundly pessimistic, the universe, as Paul Valéry's Serpent says, is a flaw in the purity of nonbeing. And so life has an ambiguous attitude toward itself: is it to be affirmed with full and simple heart, or is it itself a defect in the purity of death and nothingness? The doubt that life conceals in its own heart concerning itself is ancient: one of the earliest Greek philosophers, who evidently had never heard how sunny and vigorous the Greeks were supposed to be, said, "Best it is never to be born; second best to die young."

From the viewpoint of life, precisely what can be the role of its great enemy, death? Is it a question of simple affirmation and negation? Do we choose either life or death, or perhaps, hesitantly, a little of each?

There can of course be no "right answer" to such a question. But perhaps there may be some profit in turning the matter over in our minds. Perhaps the opposition between life and death is not absolute; maybe they can even be friendly enemies.

In this hope, let us perform an experiment in imagination. Let us imagine ourselves immortal, living forever and ever, incapable of dying. Is this indeed the dream of life? Or doesn't it at once become a nightmare, a *condemnation* to live forever? If we were incapable of dying, would any particular moment of life have any meaning at all? Is there, in other words, not an essential and necessary connection between the value of any particular experience and our own mortality? Would anything have the slightest value if we had to be around forever, testing it again and again, endlessly repeating everything that in our own actual mortal lives can be done once and once only? Our experiment in imagination might disclose that the entire poignancy and value of whatever we do or suffer in life is necessarily bound up with our mortality; each moment is unrepeatable, unique, irreplaceable. The value of every experience is bound up with the fact that we are always experiencing it for the first *and* last time. Simple affirmation of life, taken all by itself, turns into a nightmare of endless, flat existence in which nothing retains anything recognizable as value at all. Or let us consider passion. What is the energy of passion, what gives it its intensity, except the imminence of death? It is always now or never. Without that "never," would anything rouse us to passion? The "never more" is our own felt death, the lived essence of the very life of any passion. And so if at first glance life and death look like enemies, each excluding the other, at second glance they still appear enemies, but perhaps not quite so antagonistic as we thought. Neither has any sense without the other.

It is clear, then, that two particular phenomena in life disclose their inherent dependence upon death: that value in any event which lies in its uniqueness, its unrepeatability, the fact that it can never happen again; and that energy in any passion which lends it its urgency: now or never! This is why, if simple life were granted its wish to live forever, it would be condemned to both a senseless and a passionless continuation. An immortal being would be devoid of passion and could never prize the uniqueness of any moment or of its own immortal life.

There is a third element in life that would also disappear,

and we can see what it is by asking a question: At precisely which age is life to continue forever? No doubt about it, a mighty chorus would thunder back: "Youth!" Ponce de León sought the fountain of youth, they say, and what did he find? A land he called Florida, presently graced by a bewilderment of edens—Palm Beach, Miami Beach, and all the minor meccas in between, holy cities for those too sensible now for the rites of spring at Fort Lauderdale and not yet ready for the benches standing row on row in St. Petersburg. Let us take a second look at the charms of youth. For youth does have its charms, but few who have not passed beyond them suffer from the illusion that they would remain charming forever. The deepest desire of youth itself is to get it over with as soon as possible and pass into something it envisages as "maturity"; and no sooner does it accomplish this than it too falls into nostalgia for what has gone forever. Is it indeed possible for youth to escape this dialectic? Or for that matter, can the "mature" now affirm at last that maturity is a stage that is self-sufficient, and which, if it were possible, they would willingly prolong forever? If it is characteristic of youth to see the old world with fresh eyes and enthusiasms, is it possible philosophically to see the world with fresh eyes forever, repeatedly to see things for the first time? Or is not such a dream predicated on a profound loss of memory and therefore of individuality? For indeed living things do experience a second youth when their memory for the recent past is enfeebled by senility and they enter their second childhood.

Or if this seems senseless, perhaps youth might be artificially sustained by a frantic shift of experiences or styles of experience, one succeeding another in rapid succession, each new style consigning the old one to oblivion. Is this not precisely what happens when youth desires to settle into itself for longer than its own nature permits? We now find ourselves in a world of hard rock, mod clothes, hip talk, and speed, where nothing lasts longer than a weekend at Aspen or a summer on the beach. Here the sense of each thing is exhausted in its first performance. All this is of course fresh and charming for a while, but extended beyond a critical point, it becomes the very image of the boring; it too must be gotten through on the way to the much hated "maturity."

Perhaps, then, maturity can at last wish to prolong itself forever, and rest in a settled attitude against its own forthcoming extinction? If youth is characterized through and through by a wonderful, carefree existence—that is, by the spirit of fun—maturity is characterized by taking something seriously at last, by care and caring. What does it care about? First of all, it cares about its young, who are carefree either because they cannot yet take care of themselves or because they are granted a certain vacation from care by the mature before they too must begin to care. And second, the mature care for themselves. Their decisions are no longer made in the domain of games, with only make-believe victories at stake; now one's unique and only life is the prize, and the consequences determine not merely the present, but also the foreseeable future, and even what the past shall come to mean. From the position of care, the carelessness of youth must appear trivial, since it is wholly dependent upon the care of others; and yet could care ever wish to prolong itself forever? Can the sense of care be final to existence, or must not it too long at last for a release from its own burden? If our experiment in imagination has ruled out fatigue, must care not wish, precisely because it cares, to be free at last from care, not as youth is, but only as old age is—an old age, moreover, that also must be supported by the care of the mature?

And old age? It hardly requires much argument to demonstrate that it could hardly wish to perpetuate itself, now without care, but with only its previous existence to reflect upon and the blank wall of its future to contemplate. It too finally longs to confront its old enemy, death; to get it all over with at last.

In sum, life has its internal sense only in development. The static perpetuation of any particular phase would render it at once senseless; its sense lies only in the dialectical development of its phases, each with its own value, which itself lies in self-cancellation. Without this self-canceling development, a form of spiraling finally into its absolute other, death, the entire career of existence looks senseless. Again we see that death is not simply the absolute enemy, but both an enemy and the absolute condition of meaning for life itself.

We have been looking at some features of youth in general, maturity in general, old age in general; let us take a glance now at the individual man in general, if such a thing can be imagined. There surely is some truth in the common view that we don't know who a man is until we know what he will die for; nor does *he* know who he is until he knows what he would die for. And he won't know what he would die for until he dies for it. In imagination we are all Walter Mittys; we have rushed the blazing machine-gun nest, have died heroically, and are invisibly present at our own impressive funeral, or we are magically revived to receive our Medal of Honor. Clearly our fancies of ourselves are one thing, the truths of existence another; and this particular fact is in no way obviated by a cynicism that, in trying to avoid heroics or self-inflation, pretends to such a self-deflation that no experience could debase its claims, since it has made none. Nothing is more common in war than utter verbal cynicism among men who later exhibit in their conduct what can only be called heroism. And so there is no escape from what existence itself, and only existence, can disclose: who I am is what I in fact die for—that is, what I choose to die for, even when such a "choice" is not to be understood as a deliberate or reflective weighing of possibilities. If I do die through my choice, my death has the capacity of disclosing who I was, what I stood for unto death. If my death is not chosen, but is accidental, as in an automobile accident, then indeed it has no sense, is accidental to the sense of my life precisely because it was *not* chosen. And if, to take a less dramatic and more common situation, I go on until a natural and biological extinction comes upon me, then that too discloses the sense of my existence: that I did not find anything I chose to die for, that my life was not challenged by anything in it. When no such challenge has occurred, that too is an accident.

In this light suppose we look at some philosophical martyrs, beginning with Socrates. Who was Socrates? Well, as we all know, he was a Greek who thought about things, and thought about them in such a way as no one else had ever done, so far as we know. But while this is one essential meaning to his life, it is not the only one; he was also a man who, when accused by his own community of "teaching false gods," refused to alter his conviction that rational thought alone could lead to any truth worth having—precisely the conviction his fellow citizens regarded as "devotion to false gods." Socrates was, as we know, offered the opportunity to escape; his friends would have been happy to offer a bribe to the jailer, who would have been happy to accept it and let Socrates go, thus sparing the entire community the shame and embarrassment of murdering its best citizen. But Socrates refused to live under any such conditions; and so he chose his death, thinking far less of it than of betraying his own gods and living in hypocrisy. And with this choice, Socrates became Socrates, or rather disclosed who he had always been. It would be easy for us now to suggest psychological explanations of the old man's behavior; for he was indeed old, and perhaps was tired of living anyway; or perhaps he had a martyr complex and was enchanted by a vision of the figure he would cut posthumously, in the eyes of others; or, since he was not in fact anything remotely like an atheist and did argue for the immortality of a part of the soul, perhaps he wished too eagerly to taste his own immortality. But all these easy efforts to debunk Socrates presuppose that instead of being the clearest-eyed of the Greeks and of men, he was dominated by childish delusions, and far from being a sober man among drunkards, was more confused than the worst of us. Certainly Socrates did not pursue his death or welcome it, but equally certainly he did not fear it; it seems to have been rather a friendly enemy. Only because its sense could be incorporated in his life was he able to stand firm against the demands of his fellow citizens and oppose them unto death. What will a man die for? That tells us an essential thing about the sense of his life; it tells us who he is. Martin Luther at Worms, well aware of the fate of Jan Hus in a similar crisis, could say, "Here I stand, I cannot do otherwise"; and a few years later Thomas More declined his king's enticements and went joking to the headsman's block.

It should be noted also that when a man chooses his death, he is not choosing the same for all mankind; the choice is *his* death, and its sense remains essentially bound up with his unique and personal life. Socrates did not urge his students to join him in drinking the hemlock if they agreed with him. Aristotle later made a different choice, saying, "I will not permit Athens to sin twice against philosophy." Luther did not say, "Here we all stand, we cannot do otherwise," since clearly others could do otherwise and stood elsewhere. And Thomas More did not try to dissuade Reginald Pole from choosing exile, and one can imagine the jokes he would have made if he could have seen Pole later in his cardinal's hat. The sense that emerges from such stands unto death is the unique sense of each unique man's life; it is not a truth that is generalizable, or a truth for all; if it is any truth at all, it is the truth in a unique and unrepeatable life.

Furthermore, it is never an unambiguous disclosure. No sooner are such decisions made than they fall into the public domain, where their real sense becomes a matter of debate, usually to prove that the decisive event is explainable by the psychology of men who are not in the same position—men like us. We have an almost unsuppressible tendency to debunk. And yet the significance of the event does not lie in what it may or may not disclose to us; it lies in what it discloses to the man who has made the choice. It may have the function of at last disclosing to him who he has always been, or who he is here and now. When a man takes such a radical stand, a certain total significance is decided. The stand is irrevocable, it touches the totality of his existence, and it therefore puts other choices in their proper places. If we have certain ambiguities in our existence prior to any such radical choice, if we are never perfectly certain what anything means to us, whether any effort is worth the candle, whether anything we do has any consequences that are unambiguously desirable, then the choice of death clears the air. From having been distracted, dissipated, and ambiguous, each man who makes the decision chooses or decides ultimately and irrevocably what he is to be. Hence the chosen death, whether others know of it or not, touches the chooser in his own self, since no one can die for him, and may serve to disclose to him for the first time exactly where he stands. Hence living in the light of death is not an ill-chosen metaphor, nor does it connote morbidity, nor is it the product of despair, nor is it designed to weaken vitality; in short, existential thinkers are not personally responsible for the importance death may have, let alone for the fact that we all die.

The truth is that if morbidity and decadence are to be found anywhere, they are to be found in the so-called healthy attitudes, the apparently clear, simple affirmations or denials, which make sharp distinctions between life and death and opt for one or the other: the attitudes of the great optimists and the great pessimists.

Let us look for a moment at the healthy optimist, and see where his dialectic carries him. His meaning can be fixed in the image of a booming baritone proclaiming, "I love life, I want to live!" His simple message is buoyant and appealing, but it conceals tendencies that will lead him to the psychoanalyst's couch if he takes them seriously. For the optimist, the love of life is measured by the hatred and fear of death, which appears to him simply as the opposite of life and nothing more. But the more one presses the simple love of life, the more life, now appearing as the sole value and the sole condition of all value, becomes an absolute to be preserved at all costs. If my sole value is my life, there will be nothing worth dying for. How then can I avoid hypochondria? I must now become the holy guardian of the sole value I have, my own life, and the slightest threat to that value must be dodged or avoided or put off. And since it is obvious that life is never anything but a prolonged victory over its own possible dissolution, when I avoid any threat to life I am no longer a whole living being, but am caught in that paralysis which is the fear of losing life. Hence the more intensely I love life and life alone, the more certainly I lose it. I become the nursemaid of my own invalidism, an illness that I myself have precipitated by choosing the role of nursemaid.

There is a contrary simple attitude that also has a paradoxical dialectic: that of the great pessimists, who, perceiving that all things die, that death is the end of whatever makes life sweet and gives it meaning, conclude that nothing in life can have value. Since in the eternity of our nothingness our lives are but a moment, and since death will come in any event, why not pursue it now? Why wait, particularly since the time of waiting is always full of frightful pains and inevitable disappointments?

But concealed within this attitude is a most curious presupposition, one that can hardly stand the light of day: the premise that the value of an experience is some function of its duration in time. Weighed against the eternity or infinity of nothingness, no finite portion of life can have any measurable worth, since the ratio between finite quantity and infinity is itself infinite. Hence the sentiment arises that nothing in life can have sense, since no life lasts forever and no part of it lasts very long. But I have just been arguing exactly the contrary—that nothing prolonged infinitely could have value in life. If duration were indeed some measure of value, then death would have it all over life, and every rational living creature would rush to embrace it at once. And so the dialectic of the pessimists reduces them to ascribing to death a ghostly form of life, in order to *experience* the supposed value of death. The implication is not merely absurd for life; it is also absurd for the sense of death.

By refusing to entertain the paradox of death-in-life, these attitudes of absolute optimism and absolute pessimism both end in a simple affirmation, one of life and the other of death, and either affirmation turns into its opposite. The optimistic and absolute affirmation of life becomes a living death of paralysis by fear; the pessimistic affirmation of death secretly attributes to death a ghostly life in order to experience the value of not experiencing at all. The simple attitudes miss the precise sense that death might have for life, an indispensable element of meaning, which life also gives to death. It is not difficult, I believe, to detect more than a trace of these simplistic attitudes in philosophies of naturalistic vitalism, which can see in death nothing but the ashes of life, its old enemy. They are visible too in philosophies or religions of supernaturalism, which also, in their way, hardly take death seriously; why indeed take it seriously if it is only a point on an ever-lasting continuum of life that extends beyond the grave? Death is then not a final termination, and the dead are only sleeping, or have "passed on."

The dialectical relationship between life and death, in which each gives meaning to the other, is preserved in modern times in philosophies of human existence such as that of Hegel and contemporary existentialists, who have preferred to elucidate the paradoxical rather than explain it out of existence.

The sense that death can confer upon life is thus decisive. Since I must certainly die, each moment of life is unrepeatable and conclusive. It will not occur again, nor will my life occur again; and therefore each has a unique significance. Popular wisdom grasps the point in the phrase "Don't do what you wouldn't be caught dead doing," because we shall most certainly be caught dead doing something; and in point of fact, since we are always dying as well as living, we are always being caught dead doing something. Thus, only a life essentially married to death could have the sense ours does. Life might factually be extended forever, but then it would no longer be recognizably ours; it would only be the senseless continuation of an unendurable process.

Now we need only ask ourselves what it can be whose life and death are so inextricably tangled together that either becomes senseless without the other. It obviously cannot be anything whose entire nature is exhausted in its vitality, or anything whose essential significance is sheer death, or non-entity. Could it be anything but the transcendental ego, which is enacting and presiding over the whole affair?

INDEX

Accidents. *See* Events, accidental.

Actions, 23–24, 25–26; choice of, 36–37, 45 (*see also* Intentionality); existence of ego during, 63–65; objects of, 46–47; reasons for, 46; as response to world, 38–39. *See also* Consciousness, acts of; Movements.

Age, 219–220

Ambiguity: in attitude toward death, 216, 223; in horror, 209–212

Aristotle, 17; and absolute ego, 176; and death, 222; and reality, 100; and universality, 11; and values, 190; and wonder, 70

Arts: and expressiveness, 33; and horror, 200; and value, 179–180, 195. *See also* Literature; Poetry.

Attention, of ego to self, 63

Attitude, natural, 59

Autobiography, ontological, value of, 18

Becoming, 23–26

Being, 112; absolute, 175; *qua* being, 131–132; time as a mode of, 128. *See also* Existence; Ontology.

Bergson, Henri, 126, 145, 206

Binswanger, Ludwig, 111

Birth, phenomenological view of, 44

Body, physical, 107–108, 110

of, 45; ignored by philosophy, 33; mundane dimension of, 64–65; in phenomenology, 42–45. *See also* Self.

Emotions, 121. *See also* Fear; Love; Moods.

En soi, domain of, 64

Engrossment, of the ego, 72–76

Errors: in judgment, 27, 28; in memory, 153–154, 161–166

"Essences," 21

Eternity, 61; compared with time, 127–129; of consciousness, 172; of death, 225; of love, 114, 115; and memory, 159, 167, 171, 172; of the past, 170; as series of moments, 136; as theme of philosophy, 125; of values, 180

Events: accidental, 43–45, 60, 68–69, 70–72, 122, 123; explanation of, 34; past, *see* Past (*see also* Memory); singularity of, 217, 226; and time, 128–129, 137, 140

Evil. *See* Horror; Morality; Values.

Existence: choice of, by ego, 72–74; dependence of, on other existents, 176, 179; divestment of, 59, 60, 66; domain of, 69, 70, 71, 78; horizon of, 77; recovery of, 68–69; social, 78–80

Existenzerhellung (Jaspers), 35

Experience, and the absolute, 100–101

Explanation, 34–37

Expressiveness, 31, 33; and

love, 102. *See also* Communication; Language.

Failure, and horror, 203

Fear, 21, 47. *See also* Horror.

Fidelity, 26, 28; to self, 28–29

Finality, 99–100; and love, 114, 123, 124; ontological, 100; of values, 100

Freedom: and horror, 210–211. *See also* Choice, freedom of.

Freud, Sigmund: and death, 216; and horror, 208

"Fulfilled moment," 115

Fulfillment, of love, 104

Future, 47, 61, 135–136, 139

Gestalt psychology, 21

Gestures, 31. *See also* Expressiveness; Movements.

Gift-giving, 117; and morality, 195

God, 94, 95; and horror, 199; incompatibility of, with the world, 100; and morality, 189–190, 192

Good. *See* Morality; Values.

"Great Noontide," 115

Hallucination, 151

Hartshorne, Charles, 126

Hate, and love, in horror, 209–211

Heart of Darkness (Conrad), 199

Hegel, Georg, 30; and absolute ego, 176; and death, 226; and identity, 56; and love,

A NOTE ON THE AUTHOR

WILLIAM EARLE was born in Saginaw, Michigan, studied at the University of Chicago and the University of Aix-Marseilles, and is now Professor of Philosophy at Northwestern University. A man whose main interests are phenomenology, existentialism, and surrealism and the film, Mr. Earle has also written *Objectivity* and, with John Wild and James Edie, *Christianity and Existentialism,* and has translated Karl Jaspers' *Reason and Existenz.*